I0755599

MEMOIRS

OF

JOHN FREDERICK OBERLIN,

PASTOR OF WALDBACH, IN THE BAN DE LA ROCHE.

COMPILED FROM AUTHENTIC SOURCES,

CHIEFLY FRENCH AND GERMAN.

WITH A DEDICATION AND TRANSLATIONS,

BY REV. LUTHER HALSEY.

NEW YORK:
ROBERT CARTER & BROTHERS,
No. 530 BROADWAY.

1857.

DEDICATION.

O MY YOUNGER BRETHREN IN THE MINISTRY OF THE GOSPEL.

I COULD wish that we might ever set up as our model, the ministerial character of our blessed Lord and the Apostles. The more closely these are studied and copied, the more perfect and effective will be our ministry. Yet when their history is read, as there was so much that was peculiar and extraordinary, we are not enough inclined to contemplate them as models for present ministerial character. But when a successful pastor of modern times is exhibited, we feel that we are contemplating "a man of like passions with ourselves," whose example is imitable—that, in like circumstances, what he has done, we may accomplish. This disposition to admit the claims of modern examples, has induced me to desire that the Memoirs of Pastor OBERLIN should be republished, and thus find their way to the study and heart of American pastors. One thing, belonging to these memoirs, is adapted to render them signally useful beyond most other pieces of clerical biography. While in their subjects there is often a splendor of genius, a fortunate combination of circumstances, or some peculiarity in the direction of Christian exertion, which, not belonging to us, therefore discourages or forbids competition—we feel that we are not fairly matched by nature or circumstances, and are excused from similar success. But the subject of this memoir is one that comes down to "the business and bosom" of every pastor. Here we see no peculiar grandeur of intellect or acquirement—no proppings of unusual circumstance to sustain him; but a pious, humble, unattended pastor, with whose intellect and attainments we feel some fellowship, entering on a field, as humble, as arduous, as unpromising as ours; yet, in the exercise of such resources as we may command, trans forming a wilderness into a garden of the Lord. Memoirs like this, instead of discouraging, make the reader conscious of new powers, diminish the influence of impediments, and strengthen the hope of success in our own field of moral effort. The mind that does not rise from this memoir excited and mightier for God, has a heartlessness and apathy none will covet. Among the peculiar benefits derived from this memoir, I may mention the idea the reader will receive,

First, Of the comprehensiveness of the ministerial office. Too commonly this office is restricted to the mere business of preaching, and administering the sacraments. These are indeed divinely appointed and important; but even these lose much of their efficacy without the aid of external circumstances. The early Apostle, when he rose to preach, was attended by that interesting recommendation as "a man of God," the wondrous miracles he wrought. This collateral qualification gave impressiveness to his address. When the modern Apostle would preach with due impressiveness, he too needs the collateral aid derived from the character of "a man of God." This character cannot be furnished by miracle—that has ceased; nor by apostolical succession—that requires proofs; but, his character as a man of God must be evinced by those "fruits of the Spirit," the purity, the benevolence, the usefulness of his life. The preaching that is carried home by such collateral aid, will and must be heard. Such a pastor, whose active benevolence reaches the necessities of young and old, the ignorant, unskilful, sick, poor, and friendless, "with a godliness that is profitable unto all things," will interest the cold and careless, silence the penurious and gain-saying, and triumph over all opposition to the kingdom of our Lord. Such a pastor was Oberlin. Such, required at all times and places, are peculiarly necessary to our country Ours are a people that move not in the dull, mill-horse circle of prescription; they think, judge and act for themselves. Enterprising, laborious, jealous, and calculating, they will judge of ministers by their character, of character by its worth. We must therefore prove ourselves worth something to society. It is not enough that we are officially sacred and negatively good—we must be vigilantly, actively, efficiently, universally and constantly, the benefactors of our race. This is the genius of Christianity. Such was our blessed Lord, not a mere preacher, but one that "went about continually doing good." Such is the very law of our profession—"whatsoever things are true, whatsoever things are honest, whatsoever things are just, whatsoever things are pure whatsoever things are lovely, whatsoever things are of good report, if there be any virtue, and if there be any praise, *think on these things.*" [Phil. 4: 8.]

A *second* lesson of value, furnished by these memoirs, is, the striking exhibition they give, that *a parish, no matter how obscure, ignorant and poor, contains work and reward sufficient for a Christian pastor.* Such parishes none should despise. Let them rather be coveted by those men who, possessed of the benevolent heroism of Paul, desire not to "build on another man's foundation." The post of hardship is the post of honor among enterprising and patriotic soldiers—why not among the servants of Christ, "who war a good warfare?" Every inch of Satan's empire in this world has been given by grant to our Redeemer, and must be gained to him by the moral energies of his people. If it must be gained by some, why not by us? Think not that duty calls us only to work the cultivated field, when the "wilderness and solitary place might be made glad." Not only is this "covenant of promise" for our encouragement, but the history of Stouber and Oberlin evinces, that a parish secluded, rough, barbarous and poor, furnishes scope for all the piety, talents, and attainments of a pastor; all the Christian co-operation and aid of his family and friends; is compatible with the moral and intellectual improvement of his children; is adequate to his and their support; admits of the purest and warmest friendships that can cheer us in our pilgrimage, and the attainment of a reputation and influence by which a man may reach to distant countries and bless the world. The name, example, and work of Oberlin will live, when a hundred pastors of Strasbourg and Vienna, Lyons and Paris, will be forgotten!

A *third* important lesson will be strikingly exhibited in these memoirs: that the *religious state and improvement of a parish are much dependent on physical circumstances.* Unskilful husbandry, neglect of mechanic arts, badness of the roads, (beside rendering the people subject to want and famine,) prevent religious and kindly intercourse, render them incapable of sustaining schools, reading and procuring the law of the Lord, supporting and enjoying the means of grace, and by sharing their substance to the family of Christ, growing in the sentiments of Christian benevolence. The politician will therefore study to improve the resources of a country from motives of political economy; the minister of the gospel will engage in this work, because it is indispensable to moral happiness and improvement in the kingdom of the Lord on earth. Not to concern ourselves in the physical and intellectual advancement of our people, evinces a want of philanthropy, or of enlargedness of mind to comprehend the providential government of God. It is just that we should suffer for our imbecility or apathy. Let us know, and feel, and attempt our duty, watching, however, as to motives, "that whatever we do, all is done for the glory of God."

A *fourth* lesson, strongly impressed by these memoirs, is, *the true philosophy of laboring constantly and mainly for the young.* Supported by the aged, finding them our companions, and addressing their understandings from the desk, there is a tendency to overlook the youth. Hence the fact, that notwithstanding constant and labored preaching, so many congregations are stationary or even retrograding. The lambs are the future flock, and the Master's charge is, "feed my lambs." He accepted and defended the "hosannas" of the children in the temple. He vindicated their claim to his regard when apostles opposed, and left to his church this solemn and ever-binding declaration, "*Suffer* them to come unto me, and forbid them not, for of such is the kingdom of heaven."—In childhood the character of the man is forming. Then the sensibilities are most impressible, the memory most tenacious, and mind most wakeful, active, and avaricious of improvement. Then time for moral and intellectual cultivation is most in their power. Years will soon bring with them cares and embarrassments, so that they will be no longer masters of their time or of themselves. We might be instructed by the enemies of truth and righteousness. How soon do they begin the policy of error and destruction! As soon as a passion can be kindled, or a prejudice against the truth excited, the young are appealed to, and engaged. Let us, then, make the *youth* of our congregations the objects of constant regard, labor, and prayer, that they may "remember their Creator in the days of their youth," and form the noblest characters for time and for eternity. Thus will our labors be most rewarded by the constant advance of intelligence, industry, and moral feeling, not only among the young, but among the aged who will be influenced by the improvement; and when the days of feebleness shall come upon us, we and our work will be sustained by the piety, intelligence, activity, and filial affection of the young.

A *fifth* lesson from the history of Oberlin is, that *our own disinterestedness and usefulness will be the best security for our support*—a security that will triumph over every revolution and disaster. The retaliatory principle in human nature, is applied to virtue as well as vice. "With what measure ye mete, it shall be measured to you again." When the pastor himself exhibits a generous spirit, and though his resources be small, yet freely shares them for another's good, the people, while they yield more to the influence of his precepts, from this evidence of their sincerity, are by natural justice apt to reward the kindness he has bestowed. In reference to the administration of Providence, the principle is the same. The man that trusts in the Lord, and does good with a self-denying spirit, shall verily be fed. While the man that "liveth to himself," is often left of God to mourn the loss of property and influence, as well as find in man a stinted charity in the hour of calamity. The life of Oberlin had been one of self-denial, liberality and usefulness; and in the time of his changes and privations, his people were prompt and faithful to share their morsel with their kind and valuable pastor.—But I have already detained you too long from the pleasure and profit of the volume I introduce, which was, in the Providence of God compiled by an English author from unquestionable documents, for the very purpose of carrying on the valuable schools which Oberlin began. May the blessed Lord whom we serve, make us fruitful, "always *abounding* in the work of the Lord." This is His will, and the sincere prayer of

Your brother

In the Gospel and hope of Jesus,

LUTHER HALSEY

Western Theological Seminary,
October, 1830.

CONTENTS.

CHAPTER I.

CHAPTER II.

CHAPTER III.

CHAPTER IV.

CHAPTER V.

CHAPTER VI.

CHAPTER VII.

CHAPTER VIII.

CHAPTER IX.

CHAPTER X.

MEMOIRS

OF

JOHN FREDERICK OBERLIN.

CHAPTER I.

Preliminary remarks—Account of the Ban de la Roche—Its state previous to M. Stouber's time—Stouber's exertions there.

The memoirs of an individual, whose whole life has been devoted to pious and disinterested exertions for the temporal and spiritual good of mankind, have not unfrequently proved the means of awakening the desires, and strengthening the resolutions of others to follow him in his career of benevolence.

Such an individual was John Frederick Oberlin, a person whose indefatigable efforts for upwards of fifty years, to benefit the simple villagers who constituted his flock, entitle him to universal esteem and admiration. The writer earnestly hopes that the recital of his labors may, under the divine blessing, tend to confirm the zealous and encourage the weak, and lead all who hear it to catch a portion of that sacred glow by which he was himself animated.

His character, as displayed in the uniform tenor of his life, presented a remarkable combination of varied excellencies; for whilst much exalted sanctity and intrepid zeal were conspicuous, an unwearied ardor in doing good, and an habitual willingness to renounce his own interests to promote the well-being of his fellow-creatures, were equally evident. In addition to this, his extreme simplicity, conscientious integrity, sweetness of temper, and refinement of manner, caused him to be both ardently loved and sincerely revered; whilst his industry, his agricultural skill, his knowledge of rural and domestic economy, and the energy with which he carried his plans into effect the moment he was convinced of their utility, rendered him not only an example but a blessing to the people among whom he resided, and afforded a delightful proof of the advantages that may accrue from a union of secular and spiritual duties.

Before I proceed with my narrative, it will be proper to present the reader with some description of the Ban de la Roche, the scene of Oberlin's long and useful labors, and to state what had been previously effected there by his predecessor, M. Stouber, a Lutheran minister of congenial spirit with himself.

The Ban de la Roche, or Steinthal,* derives its name from a castle called *La Roche*, round which the Ban, or district, extends. It is a mountainous canton in the north-east of France, between Alsace and Lorrain, forming part of the declivities and western ramifications of the Haut Champ, or Champ de Feu, an isolated range of mountains, detached by a deep valley from th eastern boundary of the chain of the Vosges. It consists of two parishes: the one is Rothau; the

* *Steinthal* is the German name for the *Ban de la Roche.* Its literal signification is the *Valley of Stone.* —Dr. Steinkopff.

other, including three churches, comprises the five hamlets of Foudai, Belmont, Waldbach, Bellefonte, and Zolbach. These last mentioned are almost exclusively inhabited by Lutherans.

The Champ de Feu, as its name implies, bears traces of volcanic origin. It is higher than Snowdon, rising 3600 feet above the level of the sea. The village of Waldbach, at which Oberlin resided on account of its central situation, stands upon its acclivity, at the height of 1800 feet; and the usual road from Strasbourg thither lies through the towns of Molsheim, Mutzig, and Schirmeck. Behind the little town of Schirmeck the extensive and fertile valley in which it is situated, separates into two smaller ones: the well-wooded vale of Framont on the right, and that of the Ban de la Roche, of which Rothau is the first and principal parish, on the left. The approach to the latter place is romantic in the extreme; the road winding down the side of a steep precipice towards the southern side of the valley, where, after crossing the stream, which flows through its bottom in the character of a mountain torrent, it rises again, and the cottages of the peasantry become visible, partly embosomed in plantations of pine, and beneath immense masses of overhanging rocks.*

* The mountains of the Ban de la Roche are composed of granite, porphyry, and argillaceous schistus, which are commonly even with their convex surface: sienite, trapp, and grundstein, projecting on the sides and summits in irregular columns, and pointed cliffs, appear originally to have formed the general covering.

These rocks exhibit great variety in their grain and constituent parts. The granite, which is coarse, and less

The hamlet of Foudoi, at the distance of two miles from Rothau, is next in course, and occupies an almost equally picturesque situation. It is succeeded by Walbach, whose tapering spire and straw-thatched cottages are surrounded by orchards of pear and cherry trees, and by the intermingled foliage of the alder, the ash, and the sallow. The temperature varies extremely, according to the height and position of the districts. On the summits of the mountains, for instance, the climate is as intensely cold as at Petersburgh though in the valleys below it is so soft and delightful as to resemble that of Geneva, and parts of the Jura. The winter months generally commence in September, and the snow usually remains undissolved till the following May or June, when the wind blows from the south, thus leaving only a period of four or five months for summer weather. The produce of the canton necessarily varies with the elevation of the several communes; the highest are cultivated notwithstanding, though to so little purpose, that it is said the wife can carry home in her apron all the hay her husband has mown in a long morning. The harvest differs in time as well as in quantity. At Fouda, it is

---

compact towards the base of the mountains, presents the fineness of marble about 2500 feet above the valley; in these regions it is also found without quartz, taking the appearance of sienite or granite, according to the arrangement of the mica and feldspar.—Wilks.

For further particulars relating to the topography of this district, *See* Propositions Geologiques pour servir, &c. Par H [illegible] berlin, Doct. en Medicine. 8vo. Strasbourg 1806

about a week later, and at Waldbach a fortnight later, than at Rothau, which is about 400 feet below.

The district of the Ban de la Roche comprises about nine thousand acres (of 48,000 French feet), between three and four thousand of which are covered with wood, two thousand are occupied with pasture, one thousand five hundred are employed in meadows or garden land, and the remaining fifteen hundred only are cultivated with the plow.*

In the reign of Louis XV. the whole of this territory was in a most desolate state ; for having been partially the seat of conflict during the thirty years' war (terminated in 1648,) and again in the time of Louis XIV. it was so laid waste as to be scarcely habitable, there being no road from one place to another, and but little land under cultivation. About eighty or a hundred families earned indeed a scanty subsistence on its precarious soil, but, being destitute of all the comforts of civilized life, they existed in a state of misery and degradation, more easily conceived than described.

This remote district partook, however, with the rest of Alsace, in a privilege denied to the ancient French provinces. When it was incorporated with France, it was stipulated in the decree that its inhabitants should continue to enjoy the entire liberty of conscience: and whilst the persecuted Protestants of Languedoc, and other parts of France, could not find a sufficiently secure retreat for the celebration of

---

* 4 or 500 potatoes, 600 rye, 4 or 500 oats—1500.

their worship, here they possessed their own churches, and no restraint was laid upon their religious assemblies.

When M. Stouber, therefore, (who has been already mentioned as the predecessor of Oberlin,) entered upon his ministerial duties, in 1750, he had not to proclaim the "glad tidings of salvation" in the midst of intolerance and persecution, nor had he to apprehend any danger from the subtleties of theological controversy on the part of a people almost entirely destitute of the means of religious instruction. Many difficulties, however, stood in his way, in consequence of the deplorable ignorance and extreme wretchedness that universally prevailed—difficulties that would have baffled the endeavors of a mind less ardent and less energetic than his own.

The following anecdote will convey some idea of the state of the parish on his first arrival there. Desiring to be shown the principal school-house, he was conducted into a miserable cottage, where a number of children were crowded together without any occupation, and in so wild and noisy a state that it was with some difficulty he could gain any reply to his inquiries for the master.

"There he is," said one of them, as soon as silence could be obtained, pointing to a withered old man, who lay on a little bed in one corner of the apartment.

"Are you the schoolmaster, my good friend?" inquired Stouber.

"Yes, Sir."

"And what do you teach the children?"

"Nothing, Sir."

"Nothing!—how is that?"

"Because, replied the old man, with characteristic simplicity, "I know nothing myself."

"Why then were you instituted schoolmaster?"

"Why, Sir, I had been taking care of the Waldbach pigs for a great number of years, and when I got too old and infirm for that employment they sent me here to take care of the children."

The schools in the other villages were of a similar description; for, if the schoolmasters were not swine-herds, they were shepherds, who, in the summer, followed their flocks over the mountains, and, during the winter months, imparted to their little pupils the knowledge they possessed. This, however, was so trifling that many of them were scarcely able to read with fluency, and very few could write at all. A total want of method in teaching and of elementary books, also raised additional hindrances to the learners. If shown the commencement of a chapter in the Bible, it is reported of them that they could seldom find the end of the preceding chapter, and that even the most accomplished of the masters found it difficult to collect the sense of what he was reading, and would allow the children to say *Jesus* for *Je suis*, *canaille* for *canal*, or to make other mistakes equally egregious, without being aware of the error.

Stouber's first step, therefore, was to procure some schoolmasters willing to perform, and competent to discharge, the duties of their station. This was no easy task, for the office had sunk into contempt, and the more respectable of the inhabitants, regarding it as a disreputable trade, would on no account allow their sons to embrace it. The pastor's ingenuity, however, soon contrived to overcome this difficulty. He changed the *name* of the office, and the objection no longer existed. "Well then," said he, "let us have no schoolmasters, since that would not become people of your situation in life; but allow me to select the most promising of your young men, and to make them *superintendents*, (Messieurs les régents,) of the schools." To this proposition they readily acceded. His next business was to arrange a regular alphabet, and draw up a series of *spelling and reading lessons* for their use, which were printed at the expense of a benevolent individual of Strasbourg, who also presented Stouber with a thousand florins (about $220) that he might encourage those schoolmasters whose pupils made the most rapid progress, by giving them the interest of it annually, in addition to their salaries, which were necessarily very small.

The next want to be supplied was that of a *school-house*, and for this purpose Stouber begged that the necessary timber might be gratuitously furnished from the surrounding forests, a privilege which the inhabitants of the Steinthal generally had in their power to bestow. The following anecdote shows the persevering character of this remarkable man. In the bad state of the woods at this period the Abbé de Regemorte (royal Prætor of Strasbc. g) found an excuse for refusing the humble request for wood to build a school-house.—"But your Excellency," said Stouber, after having for a long time solicited in vain, "your Excellency will allow me to make a private collection among charitable individuals towards the erection of our new building?" This request was immediately granted. "Well then," continued the pastor, presenting his hat, "you are, please your Excellency, known as a charitable person, and I will make the beginning with you." On hearing these words the Prætor quickly forgot all the objections he had just been adducing, and gave him liberty to cut down as much wood as he pleased, under the express condition that he should dine with him every time he visited Strasbourg.

Having thus happily succeeded in procuring materials, a small building, or rather a log hut, was constructed under Stouber's direction and superintendence; but as he had found obstacles in the worldliness of the governor, so now he had to contend with the ignorance and *prejudices* of the people. They still opposed themselves to his benevolent efforts; for as schoolmasters had always hitherto been hired, like laborers, at the lowest price, the cheapest were regarded as the best, and the peasants began to fear that if an increase of knowledge were required from their candidates, there would be a proportionate increase of expense. Nor was this all; for on seeing the unconnected syllables which were proposed as lessons for the scholars, they were at a loss to comprehend their meaning, and for a lor g time opposed their introduction from the idea of some concealed heresy or divination

On perceiving, however, in the course of a few months, that by means of the new spelling-book little children were enabled to read any book that was put into their hands, their elder brothers and sisters, and even the parents them selves, astonished at the rapid progress they were making, and ashamed to remain behind, came forward, and begged to be instructed also. A system of regular instruction for *adults*, during part of the Sunday and the long evenings of winter, was consequently established, in addition to the schools.

Another great object of Stouber's solicitude was to disseminate and make known the ***Holy Scriptures***, as soon as he considered the people prepared for their reception. Hitherto they had only heard of the Bible as of a large book that contained the word of God; and when their pastor, in order to circulate the Scriptures as widely as possible, divided each of fifty French Protestant Bibles, he had procured from Basle, into three parts, and bound those portions in strong parchment, to enable him to make a more general distribution, he had some difficulty in convincing his parishioners that these thin volumes would answer the same purpose as the large book which they had been accustomed to see, and that they were equally the Word of God; still more to give them an idea of what was meant by the Old and New Testament, or a book, chapter or verse. They were not aware that the preceding minister had been in the habit of adhering to any particular text in his sermons; this, however, is not surprising, as he himself had not possessed a Bible for upwards of twenty years. No sooner, however, had Stouber placed these Bibles in the schools, with permission to the pupils to carry them home, than the Scriptures began to be read in their different *families*. Some of them even found their way to the Roman *Catholic* villages in the vicinity. The priests, it is true, strictly forbade their perusal, but this prohibition only served, in many instances, as an additional stimulus to the inquirer after truth. The people secretly procured them for themselves, and sometimes, considering their poverty, at a very high price. I might, indeed, mention many anecdotes of the eager delight with which this new and precious privilege was embraced, but it is sufficient to say that the desire of possessing it continually increased, and that the diffusion of Spiritual instruction, both in the Ban de la Roche and its environs, was beginning to be attended with the most cheering results.* A blessing also attended Stouber's discourses in the pulpit, for they were admirably adapted to the *capacity* and situation of his hearers. He endeavored in the simplest language to lead their minds to a knowledge of the happiness enjoyed by the people of God, and the means of attaining that happiness; and to convince them that, notwithstanding the poverty of their external circumstances, the Almighty would protect and bless them if they earnestly

* For one singular instance, among many others, of the avidity with which the Bible was sought at this period, *See* a letter of Oberlin's, Chap. VI

soug t to do his will. He then brought them to consider the all-important doctrines of the Cross, that we can only be regenerated by the influence of the Holy Spirit, and that we must rely solely upon the Lord Jesus Christ for pardon and redemption. In 1776, when he had resided about six years at Waldbach, he was appointed pastor to the market town of Barr on the other side of the Vosges. His parishioners, who, though still wild and uncultivated, had begun to feel the value of his instructions, expressed the greatest regret at his removal, as his intended successor was little more enlightened than his predecessors had been.

Four years afterwards Steinthal again became vacant; and M. Stouber, notwithstanding the reproaches and contempt cast upon him by many of his friends, who could not understand the principle of the love of Christ which constrained him to exchange a very profitable and respectable living in a town for a physical and moral wilderness, felt impelled to return to his beloved Steinthal. The pleasure with which this intelligence was circulated through the valley was extreme; the inhabitants of the different villages, both young and old, went to the top of the mountain, which had separated him from them, to witness his arrival and to bid him welcome with tears of grateful joy.

It was during this latter part of his residence in the Ban de la Roche, that M. Stouber's ministerial labors were so peculiarly *successful* and that, under the blessing of God, a general improvement appeared to take place.

He had resided altogether more than fourteen years in this spot, actively engaged in promoting the welfare of his flock, when he had the affliction of losing a wife to whom he was tenderly attached, and who, animated by the same spirit as her husband, had warmly participated in all his labors of love. She was buried in the church-yard of Waldbach, and the following touching epitaph adorned her monument, until it was destroyed, with many others, at the time of the Revolution:

During three years of marriage
MARGARET SALOME, wife of G. STOUBER,
Minister of this Parish,
Found at the Ban de la Roche, in the simplicity of a peaceable and useful life,
The delight of her benevolent heart, and, in her first confinement, the grave of her youth and beauty.
She died August 9th, 1764, aged twenty years.
Near this spot,
Her Husband has sown for immortality all that was mortal;
Uncertain whether he is more sensible of the grief of having lost
Or the glory of having possessed her.

Three years after this afflictive dispensation, which he bore with Christian fortitude, and just when he was beginning to rejoice in the happy transformation effected by his exertions, he was offered the station of pastor to St. Thomas's Church, at Strasbourg. He accepted it, and it was greatly feared that the Ban de la Roche would relapse into its former melancholy condition. To prevent this, he concerned himself to secure a suitable successor, and his mind fixed on Oberlin, to whom he communicated his wishes.

Oberlin perceived the emergency of the case his benevolent mind strongly felt the importance of such a field of labor; it was a sufficient inducement for him to undertake its duties that others disdained them, and the very misery and moral degradation which had to be remedied, rendered it in his eyes the more interesting; he therefore left a spot in which the brilliance of his mental powers might have attracted universal homage; and led, as he conceived, by the hand of Providence, became the successor of M. Stouber in this retired and desolate scene of exertion.

CHAPTER II.

Oberlin's birth and childhood—Instances of his early benevolence—His act of self-dedication—Influence over others—Arrival in the Ban de la Roche.

John Frederic Oberlin was born at Strasbourg, on the 31st of August, 1740. His father, a man of considerable attainments and respectability, though not in affluent circumstances, held an office in the Gymnasium of that city, and devoted his hours of leisure to the instruction of his nine children, to all of whom he was most tenderly attached. They in return looked up to him with devoted fondness, and acquiesced in his wishes rather from motives of sincere affection than filial duty, ever anticipating his desires, and anxiously promoting his happiness by every means in their power.

Notwithstanding the scantiness of his income, he was in the habit of giving each of his children a present of two pfenninge* every Saturday to spend as pocket-money in fruit or cakes; and the following pleasing anecdote, in allusion to this circumstance, is related as an early trait of the little Frederic's character:—when the tailor's or shoemaker's bills were brought home on a Saturday night, as he knew that his father, who was a man of remarkable integrity and punctuality, always liked to discharge them immediately to their full amount, without deducting, as the tradesmen frequently wished him to do, and as is the usual practice, the odd pence, he used to watch his countenance, and, if he imagined from its downcast expression that he was in want of money, to run to his savings'-box and return in triumph to empty all his little store of weekly pfenninge into the hands of his beloved parent.

But this was only one among the thousand instances of generosity and benevolence for which he was, even from his earliest infancy, so peculiarly distinguished. Self-denial ever seemed his ruling principle; and he was never so happy as when an opportunity of relieving the oppressed, or the distressed, presented itself to his notice. I shall mention some more anecdotes of a similar description, because it is interesting to trace the germ of those dispositions, which, when ripened into maturity, brought forth such remarkable fruits.

As he was one day crossing the market-place, when his little box of savings was nearly

* The smallest copper coin in the country, and not equal in value to an English farthing.

full, he saw some rude boys knock down a basket of eggs which a country-woman was carrying upon her head. The woman was in great trouble, when Frederic not only rebuked the boys with much spirit, but ran home, fetched his box, and presented her with all its contents. Another day he was passing in Strasbourg market, by the stall of an old clothes vender. A poor infirm woman was endeavoring, without success, to procure an abatement in the price of some article she appeared to be particularly desirous of purchasing. She wanted two sous to complete the sum demanded, and was on the point of leaving the stall from her inability to give them. Frederic, pretending to be engaged with something else, only waited for her retiring, when he slipped the two sous into the dealer's hand, and whispered him to call back the poor woman and let her have the gown; and then, without stopping for her thanks, instantly ran away.

He at another time saw a parish officer ill-using an invalid beggar in the street; and following the impulse of the moment, totally regardless of consequences, he placed himself in a spirited manner between what he thought the oppressor and the oppressed, reproving the former in strong terms for his inhumanity. The officer, indignant at such an interruption, wished to arrest the little fellow; but the neighbors, who knew and loved the boy, came running out of their shops to his assistance, and compelled the man to desist. A few days afterwards he happened to be walking in a narrow lane, when he saw the same person at a distance. "Shall

I run away?" thought he to himself. "No: God is with me. I relieved the poor man, and why should I fear?" With these reflections he proceeded on his way; and the officer, smiling at him, allowed him to pass unmolested.

This early horror of injustice and oppression was implanted by his parents, whose wise instructions and virtuous example were, in his case, crowned with the most gratifying success. To his pious and highly accomplished *mother* he often acknowledged himself indebted for his love of "things that are excellent," and for the desire that he subsequently felt of dedicating his talents and his powers to the good of others. She was indeed a truly admirable woman, and conscientiously endeavored to bring up her children "in the nurture and admonition of the Lord." She was in the habit of assembling them together every *evening, and of reading* aloud some instructive book, whilst they sat around the table, copying pictures which their father had drawn for them; and scarcely a night passed but, when on the point of separating, there was a general request for "one beautiful hymn from dear mamma," with which she always complied. The hymn was followed by a prayer; and thus their infant steps were conducted to Him, who has said, "Suffer little children to come unto me."

About this time, by way of relaxation, their father used to take them every Thursday evening at least during the summer months, to his family estate at Schiltigheim; and on arriving there, he would fasten an old drum to his waist, place his seven blooming boys in a line, and precede them in the capacity of a drummer making them face to right and left, and go through all the military evolutions. The extreme delight which little Frederic took in this exercise probably induced his early partiality for the military profession, for, whilst quite a lad, he would mingle with the soldiers and march with them; and, having attracted the attention of the officers by the display of his knowledge respecting sieges and battles, he obtained permission to join them in their exercises. His father, however, having destined him to a learned profession, at length interfered, telling the young soldier it was time to renounce this child's-play for study and serious labor. Frederic was of an ardent and lively temperament; but he readily coincided in his father's views, and devoted himself with the same enthusiasm to his literary pursuits, resolving to tread in the steps of his elder brother, the celebrated scholar of the same name, who was at this period pursuing his philological studies in the academy at Strasbourg.* By industry and application he soon regained the time he had lost; though indeed, his military exercises, having had the happy effect of strengthening and hardening his bodily frame, formed an important part of his preparation for the fatigues of the service which awaited him in the

* Jeremiah James Oberlin, a learned antiquary and laborious philologist. He wrote "Un Essai sur le Patois Lorrain des Environs du Compte du Ban de la Roche, 1776, petit in 8vo.," which contains some very curious notes upon ancient French, and in which he endeavors to prove that the patois is a corruption of the Latin language.

remarkable and arduous course which he was destined to follow.

The circumstances that induced him to resolve upon devoting himself to the ministry of the Gospel, are not known; but it appears from various memoranda found amongst his papers after his decease, that he was, from his very infancy, the subject not merely of pious convictions, but of holy affections towards his heavenly Father. "During my infancy and my youth," he says, "God often vouchsafed to touch my heart, and to draw me to himself. He bore with me in my repeated backslidings, with a kindness and indulgence hardly to be expressed." Even at a very early age his frequent prayer was, "Speak Lord, for thy servant heareth. O God, teach me to do thy will."

About this time, Dr. Lorentz excited a great sensation in Strasbourg, by the ardent zeal with which he preached a crucified Savior. Frederic's mother, attracted by the general report, went to hear him, and was so much struck with the powerful manner in which he set forth the grand doctrines of redemption and remission of sin, that she entreated her favorite son to accompany her on the following Sunday. Being a student in the theological class at the University, and having been warned by his superiors not to go, it was with some reluctance that he was prevailed on to accompany her. In compliance with her urgent solicitations, he however at last acceded, and was so much delighted with the evangelical truths he heard preached, that he became a regular and diligent attendant of the Doctor's sermons; and this circumstance probably contributed to strengthen his religious impressions, and to confirm him in the resolution he had made. At the age of twenty, he solemnly renewed his baptismal consecration to God by a formal covenant, agreeably to the method recommended by Dr. Doddridge, in his "Rise and Progress."* Although this interesting document differs but slightly from the original, I shall transcribe it, because it displays so remarkable a union of glowing zeal and lively faith, with humility and self-distrust.

---

* "I would urge you to make a solemn surrender of yourself to the service of God. Do not only form such a purpose in your heart, but expressly declare it in the divine presence.——Do it in express words. And perhaps it may be in many cases most expedient, as many pious divines have recommended, to do it in writing. Set your hand and seal to it, 'that on such a day of such a month and year, and at such a place, on full consideration and serious reflection, you came to this happy resolution that *whatever others might do, you would serve the Lord.*'

"Make the day of the transaction, if you conveniently can, a day of secret fasting and prayer; and when your heart is prepared with a becoming awe of the divine Majesty, with an humble confidence in his goodness, and an earnest desire of his favor, then present yourself on your knees before God, and read it over deliberately and solemnly; and when you have signed it, lay it by in some secure place, where you may review it whenever you please, and make it a rule with yourself to review it if possible, at certain seasons of the year, that you may keep up the remembrance of it."—*Doddridge's Rise and Progress of Religion in the Soul.* Chap. 17. p. 343.

A solemn Act of Self Dedication to God. Written by OBERLIN, *the* 1*st of January,* 1760, *and renewed by him the* 1*st of January,* 1770.

"ETERNAL and infinitely holy God! Under a feeling of deep humility and heart-felt contrition, I earnestly desire to present myself before thee. I well know how unworthy such a sinful worm is to appear before thy Divine Majesty, before the King of kings and Lord of lords, more especially on such an occasion as this, even to enter into a covenant transaction with thee.

"But the scheme and plan, O Father of mercies, is thine own; thou hast, in infinite condescension, offered it me by thy Son. Thy grace hath inclined my heart to accept of it. I come, therefore, to thee, acknowledging my numerous transgressions; and, with the repentant publican, strike my breast, saying, "God be merciful to me a sinner." I come, because I have been invited by the name of thy Son, and I rely entirely upon his perfect righteousness. Be pleased, I entreat thee, for his sake, to pardon my ingratitude, and no more remember my sins. Be reconciled, I beseech thee, to thy disobedient creature, who is now convinced of thy right to him, and desires nothing so much as to belong to thee. Holy God! I this day surrender myself to thee, in the most solemn manner. "Hear, O heavens, and give ear, O earth." I this day acknowledge the Lord is my God! I this day declare myself to be of the number of his children, and that I make one of his people. Hear my words, O my God, and write in thy book that I henceforth devote myself entirely to thee. In the name of the Lord God of Hosts, I this day renounce all former lords that have had dominion over me; the joys of the world, in which I have too much delighted, and all carnal desires. I renounce all perishable things, in order that my God may constitute my All. I consecrate to thee all that I am, and all that I have; the faculties of my mind, the members of my body, my fortune and my time. Grant me grace, O Father of mercies, to employ all to thy glory, and to live in obedience to thy commands; with an ardent and humble desire to continue thine throughout the endless ages of a happy eternity. Shouldest thou be pleased to make me, in this life, the instrument of leading others to thee, give me strength and courage openly to declare thy name. Enable me not only to devote myself to thy service, but to persuade my brethren to dedicate themselves to it also.

"Grant that through the assistance of thy Holy Spirit, I may be supported in life, and kept faithful unto death. Enable me during the rest of my days to acquire that of which I stand most in need, and to amend my ways. May the things of time no longer exercise dominion over me; but may I, during the short remainder of my life, live solely to thee. Grant me grace not only to tread in the path which, I am convinced, is the best, but enable me also to be always most active in walking in it. I resign myself, and all I am and have, to thy direction, to be disposed of in whatever manner thine infinite wisdom shall see good. I leave the management of all events to thee, and say, without restriction, "Thy will, not mine, be done!" Employ me, O Lord, as an instrument consecrated to thy service. Look upon me, as constituting one of thy flock. Wash me in the blood of thy beloved Son. Clothe me with his righteousness. Sanctify me by his Spirit. Transform me more and more into his image. Impart to me, through him, all needful influences of thy purifying, cheering, and comforting Spirit; and grant that my life may be passed under the habitual sense of thy presence, O my Father, and my God! And, after having endeavored to obey thee, and do thy will on earth, take me hence at what time, and in what manner, thou shalt see good. When the solemn hour of death approaches, and I stand on the verge of eternity, grant that I may remember this covenant, and employ my latest breath in thy service. And be pleased, O Lord, when thou seest the anguish I may have to endure in my last moments, and when I may not, perhaps, have sufficient strength to recall it, to remember it too. Then, O my heavenly Father, look down with pity on thy feeble child, and enable him to struggle with death. I wish not to prescribe to thee, O my Father, in what manner thou oughtest to take me to thyself. I wish not to ask thee to preserve me from agonizing pain. No; nothing of that kind shall form the object of my prayers. What I earnestly entreat, in the name of Jesus, is, to be enabled to glorify thee in the last hours of my life, and to evidence, amidst whatever sufferings thy all-wise providence may see meet to afflict me with, patience and submission to thy holy will. Strengthen my soul; give it confidence when thou shalt call it hence; and receive it to the embraces of thine everlasting love. Admit it into the mansions of them that sleep in Jesus —into the mansions where indescribable joys will be its portion for ever. There permit it peacefully and joyfully to await the accomplishment of the promise thou hast made to all thy people—even that of a glorious resurrection, and of eternal happiness in thine heavenly presence.

"And when I am gone to the grave, if these pages should fall into the hands of any of my surviving friends, Oh, grant that their hearts may be sensibly affected; grant them grace not only to read them as the expression of my own sentiments, but to feel for themselves also what I have expressed. Teach them to fear thee, O Lord my God, and to seek refuge with me, under the shadow of thy wings, through time and through eternity; that they may partake in all the blessings of thy covenant, through Jesus Christ, the great Mediator. To Him, and to Thee, O Father, and to the Holy Spirit, be everlasting praises ascribed by the millions of redeemed spirits, and by all those other celestial beings, in whose work and blessedness thou shalt call them to share.

"My God, and the God of my fathers! Thou who keepest thy covenant, and who scatterest thy blessings to a thousand generations, I humbly supplicate thee, since thou knowest that "the heart of man is deceitful," to vouchsafe to me grace to enter into this engagement with all sincerity of heart, and to remain faithful to my baptismal covenant. May the name of the Lord be an eternal testimony, that I have signed this covenant transaction, in the stedfast and earnest desire of keeping it.

"JOHN FREDERIC OBERLIN.

"*Strasbourg*, 1*st of January*, 1760."

"*Renewed at Waldbach*, 1*st of January*, 1770."

After having completed his studies, Oberlin was ordained, but he remained for some years without undertaking any pastoral engagement, either because he did not feel himself as yet sufficiently mature for so responsible a charge, or because no situation offered itself, adapted to the view which he had formed of his own character and suitableness. Like the admirable Fletcher,* a man of kindred spirit, who refused to undertake the care of a parish because the emoluments were too large, and the duty was too small, Oberlin wished only for a station where he might find ample scope to be useful:—for having devoted himself to his Master's service, he sought neither worldly distinctions, nor worldly honors, but determined to be actuated *only* by the specific and prevailing desire of pleasing God, and of living to his glory. During this interval, which lasted from the year 1760 to 1767, he employed himself in *private teaching*, and became domestic tutor to the family of the then distinguished surgeon, M. Ziegenhagen, of Strasbourg.

* The Rev. J W. Fletcher, Rector of Madely, Eng.

Whilst in this situation he acquired that surgical knowledge, and acquaintance with medicine, which, in his subsequent life, proved so peculiarly useful, and enabled him to render such eminent services to his parishioners.

His conscientious uprightness, amiable disposition, and entire dependence upon God in the daily events of life, caused him to be held at this time in high estimation among his fellow-citizens; and the following occurrence is related, as a proof of the influence he had almost imperceptibly acquired over them.

An honest tradesman, relying on the power of Oberlin's faith, came to him one day, and, after a long introduction, informed him, that a ghost habited in the dress of an ancient knight, frequently presented itself before him, and awakened hopes of a treasure buried in his cellar; he had often, he said, followed it, but had always been so much alarmed by a fearful noise, and a dog which he fancied he saw, that the effort had proved fruitless, and he had returned as he went. This alarm on the one hand, and the hope of acquiring riches on the other, so entirely absorbed his mind, that he could no longer apply to his trade with his former industry, and had, in consequence, lost nearly all his custom. He, therefore, urgently begged Oberlin would go to his house, and conjure the ghost, for the purpose of either putting him in possession of the treasure, or of discontinuing its visits. Oberlin replied, that he did not trouble himself with the conjuration of ghosts, and endeavored to weaken the notion of an apparition in the man's mind, exhorting him at the same time to seek for worldly wealth by application to his business, prayer, and industry. Observing, however, that his efforts were unavailing, he promised to comply with the man's request. On arriving, at midnight, at the tradesman's house, he found him in company with his wife and several female relations, who still affirmed that they had seen the apparition. They were seated in a circle in the middle of the apartment. Suddenly the whole company turned pale, and the man exclaimed, "Do you see, Sir, the count is standing opposite to you?" "I see nothing." "Now, Sir," exclaimed another terrified voice, "he is advancing towards you." "I still do not see him." "Now he is standing just behind your chair." "And yet I cannot see him; but as you say he is so near me, I will speak to him." And then, rising from his seat, and turning towards the corner where they said that he stood, he continued, "Sir count, they tell me you are standing before me, although I cannot see you, but this shall not prevent me from informing you that it is scandalous conduct on your part, by the fruitless promise of a hidden treasure, to lead an honest man, who has hitherto faithfully followed his calling, into ruin—to induce him to neglect his business—and to bring misery upon his wife and children, by rendering him improvident and idle. Begone, and delude them no longer with such vain hopes."

Upon this the people assured him that the ghost vanished at once. Oberlin went home, and the poor man, taking the hint which in his address to the count he had intended to convey, applied to business with his former alacrity, and never again complained of his nocturnal visitor.

In the year 1766, the appointment of a chaplainship to a French regiment was offered to Oberlin. As the situation accorded with the military predilections he had imbibed in his childhood, and promised to open a sphere of extensive usefulness, he partly agreed to accept it, and soon afterwards left M. Ziegenhagen's employ, and commenced a preparatory course of reading. Whilst thus engaged, the curacy of the Ban de la Roche became vacant, in consequence of M. Stouber's removal to Strasbourg. No sooner had the latter decided upon taking this step, than it occurred to him, that Oberlin, with whose piety and zeal he was well acquainted, would be admirably calculated for the vacant post, and, with the view of communicating this intelligence, he went to his lodging.

It was a little attic up three pair of stairs. On opening the door, the first object that caught his attention was a small bed, standing in one corner of the room, covered with brown paper hangings. "That would just suit the Steinthal," said he to himself. On approaching the bed, he found Oberlin lying upon it, and suffering from a violent tooth-ache. He rallied him about the simplicity of his curtains, and the homeliness of his apartment "And, pray," continued he, after having taken a survey round the room, "What is the use of that little iron pan that hangs over your table?" "That is my kitchen," replied Oberlin; "I am in the habit of dining at home with my parents every day, and they give me a large piece of bread to bring back in my pocket. At eight o'clock in the evening, I put my bread into that pan, and, having sprinkled it with salt, and poured a little water upon it, I place it over my lamp, and go on with my studies till ten or eleven o'clock, when I generally begin to feel hungry, and relish my self-cooked supper more than the greatest dainties."

Stouber congratulated him on the happiness of possessing so contented a disposition; and, assuring him that he was exactly the person he had wished to find, communicated the object of his visit.

Oberlin was rejoiced at the proposition; but having nearly concluded his engagement to undertake the office of military chaplain, he would not accept the parish until a free discharge from his engagement was obtained, and until he was convinced that no candidates for clerical preferment, who had a prior claim to himself, would accept the situation.

Those two points were soon arranged, in consequence of a candidate making application for the one office, whilst the other, which offered scarcely any emolument, was left unsolicited. The Ban de la Roche, as a sphere of pastoral labor, was wholly uninviting to any, but those who, in singleness of heart, were wishing to forsake all for Christ; Oberlin, therefore, after many earnest prayers that a blessing might rest upon himself and upon the little flock committed to his charge, accompanied his new friend and patron thither, and arrived at Waldbach on the 30th of March, 1767. He was at this time in the twenty-seventh year of his age. But how much good may be done, after this period of life!

CHAPTER III.

Oberlin's first impressions on reaching Waldbach—State of the parish—Improvements needed—Opposition manifested by the peasantry—Correspondence with M. Stouber—Letters from the latter—His marriage, and prayer—Improvements in the condition of the roads—Agricultural improvements, &c.

On Oberlin's arrival at Waldbach, he took up his residence in the parsonage house, a tolerably commodious building, formerly occupied by M. Stouber. It had a court-yard in front, and a good garden behind, and stood in a delightful situation very near the church being surrounded by steep dells clothed with wood, and rugged mountains, the tops and sides of which were partially covered with pines, and a few other straggling trees.

The first glance which he threw over the mountains destined to be the scene of his ministerial labors, convinced him, that notwithstanding the partial reformation effected by M. Stouber's exertions, neither the necessities of his flock, nor the difficulties which opposed their removal, were of any ordinary kind.

They were alike destitute of the means of mental and social intercourse; they spoke a rude *patois* resembling the Lorrain dialect, and the medium of no external information; they were entirely secluded from the neighboring districts by the want of roads, which, owing to the devastation of war and decays of population, had been so totally lost, that the only mode of communication, from the bulk of the parish to the neighboring towns, was across the river Bruche, a stream thirty feet wide, by stepping stones, and in winter along its bed; the husbandmen were destitute of the most necessary agricultural implements, and had no means of procuring them; the provisions springing from the soil were not sufficient to maintain even a scanty population; and a feudal service, more fatal than sterile land and ungenial climate, constantly depressed and irritated their spirits.

Confident, however, that strength would be afforded, if rightly sought, Oberlin at once resolved to employ all the attainments in science, philosophy, and religion, which he had brought with him from Strasbourg, to the improvement of the parish and the benefit of his parishioners.

Those individuals over whom M. Stouber had gained an influence, silently acquiesced in the projects of his successor; but a very determined spirit of *opposition* soon manifested itself among the opposite party, under the supposition that old practices are always safe, and that whatever is new must be pernicious. They resolved therefore, not to submit to innovation, but to try what they might be able to effect by determined resistance. On one occasion, soon after his arrival, they laid a plan to waylay their new minister, and inflict upon him a severe personal castigation, judging that such a measure, at the commencement of his career, would prevent his future interference.

Oberlin happily received information of their intention, and, without being disconcerted at the intelligence, immediately determined upon a mode of correction, in which the peculiar gentleness and decision that formed such leading traits in his character were remarkably displayed.

Sunday being fixed upon for the execution of this attempt, when the day arrived he took for his text those words of our Savior, in the fifth chapter of St. Matthew:—"But I say unto you, that ye resist not evil; but whosoever shall smite thee on thy right cheek, turn to him the other also;" and proceeded from these words to speak of the Christian patience with which we should suffer injuries, and submit to false surmises and ill usage. After the service the malcontents met at the house of one of the party, to amuse themselves in conjecturing what their pastor would do, when he should find himself compelled to put in practice the principles he had so readily explained. What then must have been their astonishment, when the door opened, and Oberlin himself stood before them!

"Here am I, my friends," said he, with that calm dignity of manner which inspires even the most violent with respect; "I am acquainted with your design. You have wished to chastise me, because you consider me culpable. If I have indeed violated the rules which

I have laid down for you, punish me for it. It is better that I should deliver myself into your hands, than that you should be guilty of the meanness of an ambuscade." These simple words produced their intended effect. The peasants, ashamed of their scheme, sincerely begged his forgiveness, and promised never again to entertain a doubt of the sincerity of the motives by which he was actuated, and of his affectionate desire to promote their welfare.

A few weeks after this event another circumstance, of a similar nature, occurred in one of the adjoining villages. He was informed that the young people belonging to it had determined to seize him the following Sunday, on his leaving their place of worship, and duck him in a cistern. He consequently took occasion to speak, in his sermon, of the happiness and security enjoyed by those who trust in the Lord; of the special protection which he vouchsafes to his servants; and of his firm belief that not a hair of our heads can be injured without his express permission. He was in the general habit of returning home on horseback, but this time he set out purposely on foot, desiring a peasant to lead his horse. He had not proceeded far, before he saw two or three men partly concealed behind the hedge, and awaiting his approach. He passed them, however, with so calm and composed a countenance and step, that they were daunted, and did not venture to put their plan into execution.

These occurrences are believed to have had a good effect in accelerating the execution of his projects of reform; for those who had connived in the plots against him, anxious to reinstate themselves in his good esteem, and conscious that they had no better means of succeeding than by warmly seconding the views which they had hitherto opposed, were henceforward among the foremost to assist him.

During the first years of his residence in the Ban de la Roche, Oberlin found an enlightened and experienced guide, and a wise and faithful counsellor, in his predecessor, M. Stouber. The following letter, addressed by the latter to his young friend, is full of excellent counsel and advice; and proves that he had himself felt the responsibility attached to so peculiar a situation:

"*Strasbourg, June 2d,* 1768.

*   *   *   *   *

*   *   *   *   *

"Do not, my dear friend, suppose that I could have done any thing better than you have done it. God alone can enable either of us to do just so much as he pleases, and no more. The little experience that it cost me long years of labor and difficulty to obtain, you will acquire more speedily. You possess it already in some degree, though still insufficiently. When I was in your situation, a single circumstance, or even a single word, would sometimes discourage and discompose me so much that I did not know what to do. I could not help perceiving almost every day that I had ignorantly committed the greatest mistakes—ignorantly escaped the greatest dangers—ignorantly lost or acquired the greatest advantages:—

that what I sought was evil, and what I shunned good;—that what I hoped for was nothing and what I supposed nothing, something. If it was God's purpose that any scheme of mine should succeed, he caused the heads of the parish to listen to me even when I least expected it, and had made the least preparation for it; and, as frequently permitted the plans upon which I had grounded my hopes of success, and taken the most pains to carry into effect, to become of no avail.

"In so deplorable a state are the people of the unfortunate Steinthal, that one in your situation can do nothing but commend them to God, and look for succor and assistance from him alone. If he should see meet to let things go on for a period in their present state, and without any visible improvement, do not be discouraged. He undoubtedly will, in his own good time, effect such changes among some of the members of your flock, as neither the folly nor the taunts of the remainder, nor the craft and malice of the enemy, shall be able to subvert; and whilst you trace his finger throughout the whole, and thank him for having crowned your exertions with even this partial success, you will find increased cause for the exercise of self-distrust, patience, and humility. God will, I feel assured, bless your endeavors, if you continue to maintain that *devotedness of spirit*, which your letter so sweetly and fervently breathes. Only trust every thing to him; and pray for the blessing which he alone can bestow. You have more influence over others than I have; and this, provided you fear no one but God, and guard against forming too many schemes, will render you in truth more useful than I have been. But I must remind you, that, even when deeply engaged in good works, it is possible to depart from *spiritual* Christianity; and I would, on this account, urge you to maintain a constant guard over yourself. You have been brought under the influence of religion, and, in the usual sense of the term, converted to God; but, without constant prayer to him, and the most zealous watchfulness, there is a danger lest you should rest satisfied with this, and relapse into indifference. By being so incessantly occupied in the prosecution of your favorite schemes, and destitute of stimulating society, you may become cold and lukewarm in your religious duties, and less devoted in your service to God, even though busily employed in promoting the well-being of your fellow-creatures. I would, therefore, earnestly exhort you, my dear friend, to be always "fervent in spirit, serving the Lord," living only to, and for, Him. Thus you will be enabled to overcome difficulties; you will find comfort and peace in believing, and He will protect, guide, and bless you. Your work will prosper, not perhaps in the manner which you design, but in the way which God has purposed.

"I have no other end in view in this exhortation than your good. I wish you to understand that this is, literally, my only object in writing thus plainly. I speak frankly and sincerely to you, because I know that our hearts are closely allied, and because I have sometimes observed with deep concern the dangers incident to young persons; coldness and lukewarmness after the first fervor of religious feeling has subsided; *self-sufficiency* in what they have effected, and too great tendency to *absorption* of mind in even laudable and benevolent pursuits.

"This is the motive that induces me, once for all, to warn you on this point; for the heart of man is deceitful, and naturally tends to earth, if it is not constantly drawn upwards.

"There are yet two things to which I particularly wish to direct your attention;—*prayer* and the *Holy Scriptures*. I find it necessary, in order to keep up habitual communion with God, and to fan the spirit of Christianity in my own bosom, to have constant recourse to them.

"It is by reading the writings of the Apostles, almost exclusively, that I am enabled to press onward in my spiritual course, and to encourage myself to prayer.

* * * * *
* * * * *

"Yours, my dear friend,
"In the bonds of Christian love,
"G. STOUBER."

Warned and encouraged by such powerful xhortations, Oberlin went on his way rejoicing, and eventually became established in Christian faith and holiness.

But I have now to speak of an event which materially contributed to enhance his temporal happiness. This was his marriage with a very pious and amiable young lady of Strasbourg, named Madeleine Salomé Witter.

Previous to his settlement in the Ban de la Roche, his mother had anxiously desired to see him united to one who would participate in his labors, relieve him from domestic cares, and cheer and solace him in the remote and lonely situation in which he was about to be placed. He, however, was easy on the subject, but, out of regard to his parents, agreed to accede to their wishes, provided they could select a suitable companion for him. Mrs. Oberlin had been told, in confidence, that her son would probably meet with success by asking the hand of the daughter of a rich brewer's widow. He was persuaded to try his fortune in person; but as it had, from early youth, been a principle with him to wait for some intimation from Providence, whenever his reason proved an insufficient guide, he earnestly prayed that God would be pleased to reveal his will to him, and to direct him in his judgment, whether the marriage would be likely to conduce to his happiness, by the manner in which the mother should receive him. If she should herself make the proposition, he resolved to regard it as a sign of providential approbation; but, if not, to consider it his duty to abstain from mentioning the subject. He then proceeded towards the house, and rang the bell. The mother gave him a courteous reception, and even called down her daughter, whose appearance did not, however, particularly please him; they sat down talked of a pretended cause of the visit, of the weather, and of the news about the town, till at length all topics being exhausted, a silence succeeded; the parties looked at each other in some surprise, for Oberlin was a novel visitor there, and then looked down again. This scene of "silent state" lasted about two minutes, when the latter, who had decided in his own mind how to act, made a polite bow, opened the door, shut it again, and took his departure, leaving both mother and daughter at a loss to conjecture the cause of this singular visit, and the marriage was never again thought of. The apprehensions of his fond parents were, however, continued. They had long maintained a friendly intercourse with the family of Frederic's former schoolmaster, and he was himself warmly attached to the person of the latter. He had one daughter, a young woman of an agreeable disposition, for whom Oberlin had long entertained a cordial esteem. With his consent the parents drew up a preliminary marriage contract between them; but a more wealthy suitor was finally preferred by the family of the schoolmaster, and this circumstance induced the young lady to withdraw from the contract. A few weeks only had elapsed after this circumstance, when Oberlin received a note from her father expressing a wish to renew the connexion. Upon its receipt he immediately repaired to the schoolmaster's house, with the note in his hand, which he returned, saying, "My dear Sir, I am accustomed to follow the intimations of Providence. I consider what has recently occurred, as an intimation that a marriage between your daughter and myself would neither tend to her happiness, nor to mine. Let us, therefore, say no more about it, and forget all that has passed. Allow me again to participate in your affection, as I can assure you that mine has not been in the least diminished; nor have I lost a particle of the gratitude I owe you, for all your instructions."

He then continued the conversation on general subjects, and the intercourse between the two families remained undisturbed.

These two plans having successively failed, Mrs. Oberlin yielded to the wishes of her son, and allowed him to set out for his parish. She, however, accompanied him to Waldbach, and assisted in arranging his domestic establishment, the care of which devolved on his younger sister, Sophia. About a year after his settlement there, Miss Witter, who was a friend and relation of the family, came to pay a visit in the Steinthal, and stopped some weeks at the parsonage. She had lost her father, who was a professor in the University of Strasbourg, at a very early age, and her mother died shortly afterwards; but although deprived of the benefit of parental instruction, she possessed a sound understanding, and a highly cultivated mind, deeply imbued with religious principles.

She was, however, at this time, more expensive and worldly in her habits than her cousin Frederic, and their dispositions did not entirely harmonize.

The time of her departure at length drew near. Only two days before the period fixed upon for her return to Strasbourg, Oberlin felt as though a secret voice within, whispered,

"Take her for thy partner!" He, however, resisted the call. "It is impossible," said he, almost aloud,—"our dispositions do not agree." "Take her for thy partner!" the voice still continued. He spent a sleepless night, and, in his prayers the next morning, solemnly declared to God, that if he would give him a sign, by the readiness with which Madeleine should accede to the proposition, that the union was in accordance with his will, he would cheerfully submit to it, and consider the voice he had heard as a leading of Providence.

After breakfast, the same morning, he found the young lady sitting in a summer-house in the garden. Placing himself beside her, he began the conversation by saying, "You are about to leave us, my dear friend;—I have had an intimation that you are destined to be the partner of my life. If you can resolve upon this step, so important to us both, I expect you will give me your candid opinion about it before your departure."

Upon this Miss Witter rose from her seat, and, blushing as she approached him, placed one hand before her eyes, and held the other towards him. He clasped it in his own. The decision was made:—a decision which he never found cause to regret, for, notwithstanding the determination Madeleine had made not to be allied to a minister, she became truly devoted to his interests, and the most cordial attachment ever after subsisted between them.

The marriage took place July 6th, 1768.

The following affecting prayer, written by Oberlin at this period, will give some idea of the feelings with which, in conjunction with those of his affectionate partner, he entered into the sacred engagement, and also of the spirit which ever afterwards pervaded their peaceful household.

Oberlin's Prayer on his Marriage.

"HOLY SPIRIT! descend into our hearts; assist us to pray with fervor from our inmost souls. Permit thy children, O gracious Father, to present themselves before thee, in order to ask of thee what is necessary for them.

"May we love each other only in thee, and in our Savior Jesus Christ, as being members of his body. Enable us, during the whole day, to look solely to thee, and to walk before thee, that we may be gathered together in thee, and thus become daily more spiritually minded.

"Grant that we may be faithful in the exercise of our duties, that we may stimulate each other therein, warning each other of our faults, and seeking together for pardon in the blood of Jesus Christ. When we pray together, (and may we pray much and frequently,) be thou, O Lord Jesus, the third in the midst of us. And do thou, O heavenly Father, enable us to be very fervent; and grant, for the sake of Jesus Christ, that which thine Holy Spirit shall teach us to ask.

"Seeing that, in this life, thou hast placed the members of our household under our authority, give us wisdom and strength to guide them in a manner conformable to thy will. May we always set them a good example, following that of Abraham, who commanded his children and his household, after him, to keep the way of the Lord, to do justice and judgment. If thou givest us children, and preservest them to us, O grant us grace to bring them up to thy service, to teach them early to know, to fear, and to love thee, and to pray to that God who has made a covenant with them, that conformably to the engagement which will be undertaken for them at their baptism, they may remain faithful from the cradle to the grave. O heavenly Father, may we inculcate thy word, according to thy will, all our lives, with gentleness, love, and patience, both at their rising up and lying down, at home and abroad, and under all other possible circumstances; and do thou render it meet for the children to whom thou hast only given life as a means of coming to thee.

"And when we go together to thy Holy Supper, O ever give us renewed grace, renewed strength, and renewed courage, for continuing to walk in the path to heaven; and, as we can only approach thy table four times in the year, grant that in faith we may much more frequently be there, yes, every day and every hour; that we may always keep death in view, and always be prepared for it; and, if we may be permitted to solicit it of thee, O grant that we may not long be separated from each other, but that the death of the one may be speedily, and very speedily, followed by that of the other.*

* The designs of the Lord were different, and this prayer was not answered. Oberlin, for the happiness of

"Grant us our requests, O gracious Father in the name of Jesus Christ, thy well-beloved Son. Amen. And O, merciful Redeemer may we both love thee with an ardent devotion, always walking with thee and holding communion with thee, not placing our confidence in our own righteousness and in our own works, but only in thy blood and in thy merits. Be with us; preserve us faithful, and grant, Lord Jesus, that we may soon see thee. Holy Spirit, dwell always in our hearts: teach us to lift up our thoughts continually to our gracious Father; and give us according to our need, strength and consolation. And to thee, to the Father, and to the Son, be praise, honor and glory, for ever and ever. Amen."

Mrs. Oberlin soon became an invaluable assistant to her husband in all his labors of love, tempering his zeal with her prudence, and forwarding his benevolent plans by her judicious arrangements. In the prosecution of those plans much Christian firmness was requisite, for they had, as we have already seen, to encounter the prejudices generally attendant on ignorance, and such as the most unwearied patience and self-denying virtue could alone have surmounted.

About this time she wrote the following act, renewing her baptismal covenant:

---

his fellow-creatures, lived forty-two years after the death of his wife. "My thoughts are not your thoughts, neither are your ways my ways, saith the Lord." Isaiah 55: 8.

"*Act of sincere renewing my covenant of baptism; made in presence, and in the name of the most holy Trinity, of God the Father, of God the Son, and of God the Holy Spirit.*

"As the anniversary of my baptism approach es, I ask myself if it is in the service of God that I have employed the many years of existence that he has given me; but alas! I must confess, full of shame and sorrow, that I have stolen the most precious of my time from God, and given it to the service of the god of this world; and yet I feel no shame, no grief, no true horror of the sin in my soul. Thou, my God, must operate all this in me. Thou wilt do it. Thou hast opened my eyes to the subject, to make it appear to me that I have not served thee. Thou wilt accomplish the remainder; yes, I am sure of it, and although thou hidest thyself, yet at last thou wilt make thyself known to my soul with thy divine efficacy. I dare speak, even as I have already had the proof of it.

"In the name of the most Holy Trinity, and in the presence of the holy angels, I promise that by his assistance I will consecrate to God the remainder of my life; but Lord Jesus, what have I promised? I take too much upon me, poor worm of the earth as I am; me, with my extreme coldness, who see nothing but obscurity around me and in me, still I would consecrate myself to the service of God. Yes, I would! It is there precisely that my Savior loves to manifest his name, to make clear his mercy and his infinite tenderness, where man has no more merit nor strength. Dear Savior I see nothing but evil in me; I am so much the more diseased, since I feel not even my malady.

"My Savior, thou wilt not abandon me, thou canst not but take pity on me, thy promise is clear. Thou canst not but take pity on me; thou hast given me this word in my heart, "I will be with him in trouble; I will deliver him, with long life will I satisfy him, and show him my salvation." What is this salvation but spiritual benefits? what is this long life, but the life eternal, and best happiness?

"It is from thee that I hold this gracious promise; it is thou who hast many times comforted my soul by it in afflictive events. I have it alive in my soul. When Satan would deprive me of this consolation, grant that it be powerful in my heart. Send back to the enemy his envenomed darts, that he shoots at me; grant that, conducted by thy dear Holy Spirit, I may continue my pilgrimage as a person who desires to be truly thy child, and who feels herself redeemed by thy blood.

"Behold, dear Savior, my heart and my hands; I am thine; I with my dear husband and my dear children. I will that we may be all entirely thine, soul and body; take and possess all that I have; bring us near, and arrange our hearts so that we may at all times appear in thy sight built upon thy merits only.

"If this writing fall after my death into the hands of my children or of other persons, grant that it may make a salutary impression upon their souls.

"Once more, my very dear Savior, I give myself to thee; grant me thy Holy Spirit, to conduct and govern me; give me a heart docile and obedient, and a faithful attention to thy voice. Give me the spirit of a child who loves thee, and who has not a slavish fear of thee Give me a living faith, that no unbelief may separate me from thee. To the hour of my death, dear Savior, remember thy poor servant, that thine angels may bring me even to thy throne; make me to hear then thy voice of peace and of grace, which says,—"Come, ye blessed of my Father, inherit the kingdom prepared for you from the foundation of the world." Lord God, Jesus Christ, my lovely Savior, add to all this thy precious—"yea!" Most holy Trinity, grant thy "yea," thine "amen," to my prayer.

"I have composed this act and sign it with my hand, according to the movement and the full choice of my heart.

"MADELEINE SALOME OBERLIN."

"*Waldbach*, 1777."

Almost the first object of Oberlin's provident activity was to repair and widen the *roads*. In a country where rocks hanging on the steep declivity of a chain of mountains, and rapid torrents pouring from their summits, are perpetually causing considerable falls of loosened earth, the formation and preservation of roads involve an expense far beyond the resources of a poor and isolated parish; and all the roads belonging to the Ban de la Roche were, consequently, during the greater part of the year absolutely impassable.

To rescue his parishioners from the half-savage state in which he found them, he judged it necessary, as a preliminary measure, to bring them into contact with the inhabitants of other districts, further advanced in civilization; and for this purpose to open a regular communication with the high road to Strasbourg, by which means the productions of the Ban de la Roche might find a market, and materials be procured for exercising their industry and ingenuity.

Having, therefore assembled the people, he proposed that they should blast the rocks, and convey a sufficient quantity of enormous masses to construct a wall to support a road, about a mile and a half in length, along the banks of the river Bruche, and build a bridge across it near Rothau.

The peasants were perfectly astonished at the proposition. The project appeared to them totally impracticable, and every one excused himself, on the plea of private business, from engaging in so stupendous an undertaking. Oberlin, still intent on the prosecution of his scheme, endeavored to refute the objections raised on all sides: "The produce of your fields," said he, "will then meet with a ready market abroad ; for, instead of being imprisoned in your villages nine months out of the twelve, you will be enabled to keep up an intercourse with the inhabitants of the neighboring districts. You will have the opportunity of procuring a number of things of which you have long stood in need, without the possibility of obtaining them, and your happiness will be augmented and increased by the additional means, thus afforded, of providing comforts for yourselves and your children." But his arguments were concluded with a more touching appeal. He offered them his *own example* in the undertaking. "Let all," said he, "who feel the importance of my proposition, come and work with me."

Oberlin had already traced the plan, and no sooner had he pronounced these words, than, with a pick-ax on his shoulder, he proceeded to the spot; whilst the astonished peasants, animated by his example, forgot their former excuses, and hastened, with unanimous consent, to fetch their tools and follow him. He presently assigned to each individual an allotted post, selected for himself and a faithful servant the most difficult and dangerous places; and, regardless of the thorns by which his hands were torn, and of the loose stones by which they were occasionally bruised, went to work with the greatest diligence and enthusiasm. The emulation awakened by his conduct quickly spread through the whole parish. The increased number of hands rendered an increased number of implements necessary; he procured them from Strasbourg; expenses accumulated; he interested his distant friends, and, through their assistance, funds were obtained; walls were erected to support the earth, which appeared ready to give way; mountain torrents, which had hitherto inundated the meadows, were diverted into courses, or received into beds sufficient to contain them; perseverance in short, triumphed over difficulties, and, at the commencement of the year 1770, a communication was opened with Strasbourg, by means of the new road, and a neat wooden bridge thrown across the river. This bridge still bears the name of "*Le Pont de Charite.*"

The immediate advantages resulting from this great undertaking, increased the influence which Oberlin was already beginning to acquire over his parishioners, and rendered the adoption of his successive plans, particularly that of a regular communication between the five hitherto separated villages, still more practicable. It seemed as though nothing could daunt their ardor; and the pastor, who, on the Sabbath, had directed their attention with that earnestness, and warmth, by which his own soul was animated, to "the rest that remaineth for the people of God," and to the "city which hath foundations," was seen on the Monday, with a pick-ax on his shoulder, marching at the head of two hundred of his flock, with an energy that neither fatigue nor danger could diminish.

One of the next wants that he found it necessary to supply, was a *depot* in the valley, for agricultural tools and implements of husbandry; for whenever any of them happened to break, or to get out of repair, two whole days' work must be lost in going to Strasbourg to procure more, and even then the poor peasants were destitute of ready money to purchase them. To remedy this inconvenience, he stocked a large warehouse in Waldbach with the necessary articles, and gave the purchasers credit till their payments came round. He also established a sort of lending fund, under such strict regulations, that those who did not punctually repay the money they had borrowed on the prescribed day, were deprived, for a certain time, of the liberty of borrowing again.

Another measure, which he considered essential to the progress of civilization, was the introduction of *trades*. There were neither masons, blacksmiths, nor cartwrights, in the country, and the inhabitants were subjected to numerous privations, and to great expenses, in fetching from the neighboring towns what was needful for the supply of their wants. Oberlin, therefore, selected from among the elder boys some of the readiest abilities, and sent them to Strasbourg, to learn the trades of a carpenter, a mason, a glazier, a cartwright, and a blacksmith. By this means he succeeded in procuring good workmen, who, on their return, not only instructed others in their newly acquired arts, but saved the people of the Ban de la Roche the expense and loss of time they had formerly incurred: nor was this the only advantage accruing from so judicious a step, for the money which had hitherto been sent to a distance was now circulated among themselves. So scarce had money previously been, that the gift of a single *sou* is said to have overwhelmed a poor woman with joy, as it enabled her to procure a little salt to eat with her potatoes.

Finally, Oberlin's solicitude extended to

their dwellings. They were generally wretched cabins hewn out of the rocks, or sunk intc the sides of the mountains; and without cellars sufficiently deep to preserve the potatoes, which formed their principal sustenance, from the frost. Under his superintendence and direction, however, *cellars* were constructed, and comfortable *cottages* erected.

In the prosecution of these plans, as well as those introduced at a later period, Oberlin was much indebted to the counsel and experience of his paternal friend, M. Stouber, with whom he maintained a regular correspondence. The following extract from one of his letters, deserves insertion in this memoir, because the advice it contains may prove of utility to others, as well as to the individual for whom it was originally designed:—

"My dear Friend,

* * * * *

* * * * *

"The best advice I can give you, is to care chiefly for the *souls* of your flock. I would not have you too anxious to render them eager in the pursuit of worldly good; for, as they become Christians they will naturally become active, industrious and provident. You must not allow them to be either idlers, or the slaves f mammon.

"By endeavoring too much to induce them to adopt your plans in preference to others, and on account of some supposed superiority over those to which they have been accustomed, you will defeat your own purposes, and excite their suspicion and disgust I advise you, therefore to leave them, for the present at least, pretty much to their own devices, and to labor, in charity and love, for the salvation of their souls, firmly believing that by so doing you will obtain the greatest blessing. This is the last thing that experience taught me, during my residence in the Steinthal, or rather since I left it. I must regret having occasionally induced the people to do things against their will. If I were now there, I would leave them much more to themselves; and, however indifferent might be the appearance of their external affairs, the state of their finances, or the conduct of their schools, I would say little to them on the subject of economy or management; but, by evincing a sincere interest in their concerns, I would endeavor to gain their confidence, and induce them to regard me as their friend; and then having once obtained this confidence, and a proportionate degree of influence, I would exert it to the utmost of my ability, to their advantage, both in the instruction of the young and the conversion of the old, seeking to win their affections by my earnest desire to promote their spiritual interests. If you adopt this method, my dear friend, God will take care of the rest. Necessity will compel your people to employ themselves, and they will think a thousand times better of their own schemes, than of any that you can propose to them.

"I am far from wishing you to give up your projects, (many of which have been already attended with such admirable success,) but I acknowledge that I have, for my own part, felt the danger of bestowing too much attention upon such things, rather than upon more essential and important duties. At the same time, I would not have you by any means neglect a ready acquiescence in such practical schemes as may suggest themselves to the minds of your people, or the adoption of such as may occur to yourself:—only do not make them your primary object."

Oberlin particularly felt the importance of the latter part of this advice in his efforts for the improvement of *agriculture;* a branch of rural economy in which the mountaineers, however readily they might acquiesce in his other plans, evinced great reluctance to be instructed, supposing that their own knowledge of the subject must necessarily exceed that of their pastor, whose life, previous to his arrival in the Ban de la Roche, had been generally spent in a town.

He knew this so well that he determined to appeal to their eyes rather than their ears, believing that they would be more easily led to coincide in his views when they had seen his theories reduced to practice. Belonging to his parsonage were two gardens, crossed by very public foot-paths, and these he chose for the scene of his labors. Assisted by a favorite and intelligent servant, he dug trenches, four or five feet deep, and surrounded the young trees, that he planted in them, with such soil as he considered best adapted to promote their growth. He also procured slips of apples, pears, plums, cherries, and walnuts, and made a large nursery ground of one of the gardens, hitherto noted for the poverty of its soil and then waited with patience for the time when his parishioners, observing the success of his experiments, should come of their own accord to express their astonishment, and to ask his assistance in raising trees for themselves.

His expectations were not disappointed; the rees grew and flourished; and, as the peasants had to pass through the gardens in going to their daily work, they could not help stopping to observe the surprising contrast between the scanty supply of their own, and the rich produce of their pastor's land, and at length repaired to him, anxiously inquiring how such very fine trees could grow in such a soil. Oberlin, according to his accustomed method of deriving instruction from every incident, first directed their thoughts to Him who "causeth the earth to bring forth her bud," and who "crowneth the year with his goodness," and then proceeded to explain the mode of cultivation, by which, under his all-superintending Providence, their exertions might be followed by similar success.

The taste for planting trees was thus diffused, and the art of grafting, in which he himself instructed those who wished to understand it, became a favorite employment. The very face of the country, in consequence, underwent a complete change; for the cottages, hitherto for the most part bare and desolate, were surrounded by neat little orchards and gardens; and, in the place of indigence and misery, the villages, and their inhabitants, gradually assumed an air of rural happiness.

So barbarous before Oberlin's time had been

the state of the Ban de la Roche, with regard to the most simple agricultural arts, that the old men told him they remembered to have heard from their fathers, that previous to the year 1709, the people of this canton subsisted chiefly upon wild apples and pears. The dreadful famine that took place that year, compelled them to devise means for procuring some other sustenance; and, with this view, they partially cleared away an immense forest, which extended nearly all over the country, and planted a sort of potatoes, (*quemattes*, or *cruattes de tierre* in the *patois*,) which were then first introduced. Owing to the rigorous seasons, and to the soil having been often swept away from the rocks it covered by the rain, this primitive potatoe had so far degenerated, that, when Oberlin came to the Ban de la Roche, in 1767, fields that had formerly yielded from 120 to 150 bushels, furnished only between 30 and 50. The people imagined that the ground was in fault, but no means of remedying the evil ever occurred to them. Oberlin, attributing the circumstance to its true cause, pointed out to them the means of recovering the crops, made them acquainted with Parmentier's useful work on the subject, and procured some seed from Switzerland, Holland and Lorrain, to renew the species. The sandy soil of the mountains being peculiarly favorable to their vegetation, abundance soon returned; and potatoes of a superior quality and flavor, soon became, and are to this day, celebrated as the great production of the place, furnishing not only a sufficient store for home consump ion, but also a profitable article of exportation.

Believing that great advantages would accrue from the cultivation of leguminous plants and productive herbs,* before unknown in that part of the country, Oberlin's next attempt was to raise saint-foin; but, as this plant strikes its root perpendicularly, and the soil of the Ban de la Roche is not deeper than two feet at most on the rocks and sandstone, it did not succeed, though the flax, which he raised from seed imported from Riga, and the Dutch clover, which he also introduced, answered perfectly well,

* Having acquired, during his residence in M. Ziegenhagen's family, a thorough knowledge of botany, Oberlin made his people acquainted with the properties of their indigenous plants, particularly with such as were serviceable for food, health, and the useful arts. The names of some of them will excite surprise, accustomed as we are to pass them by unnoticed. Among them were the stripe-flowered cabbage, *brassica oleracea;* common chick-weed, *stellaria media;* water mouse ear chick-weed, *cerastium aquaticum;* common goose-foot, *chenopodium bonus-henricus;* common dandelion, *leontodon autumnale;* mountain willow-herb, *epilobium montanum;* butter-cup, *ranunculus ficaria;* yellow dead nettle, *galeobdolon luteum;* white dead nettle, *lamium album;* common hop, *humulus lupulus;* red pimpernel, *anagalis arvensis;* great plantain, *plantago major;* upright crow-foot, *ranunculus acris;* twisted snake-weed, *polygonum bistorta;* common sorrel, *rumex acetosa;* lamb's lettuce, *valeriana locusta;* bladder campion, *cucubalus behen;* water-cress, *sisymbrium nasturtium;* and corn cockle, *agrostemma githago.* He taught them to mix the seeds of the latter with corn in making their black bread; and to procure a sort of wine, called *piquette*, from the wild cherry, *prunus cerasus;* juniper, *juniperus communis;* dog rose, *rosa canina*, &c. to distil brandy from elder-berries, and to obtain oil from beech-nuts.

and considerably augmented the resources of the inhabitants.

This success was probably owing in part to the attention he paid to the management of manure, which constitutes a chief secret in agriculture. He not only directed his laborers to the means of enriching it by fermentation, but taught them also that all sorts of vegetable substances, even the leaves of trees, the stalks of rushes, moss, and fir apples, might be converted into a useful compost. Acting upon his favorite maxim, "*gather up the fragments, that nothing be lost*," he also instructed children to tear old woollen rags into pieces, and to cut up old shoes for this purpose; and to facilitate their labors, he paid them sixteen sous for a bushel, and one sou for the smallest quantity they liked to collect.

These incidents may appear trifling and unworthy of record to some of my readers; but they are mentioned, together with others in the course of the narrative, as characteristic proofs of the real interest with which Oberlin entered into every thing likely to conduce to the welfare of his flock. As soon as he was fully convinced that they began to recognize the utility of his instructions, he endeavored to point out to them the advantages that would arise to them from converting the least productive pastures into arable land, and feeding the cattle in their stalls; in order to increase the quantity of milk and butter, which constituted not only so large a part of their subsistence, but also an article of commerce.

This conversion of grass into arable land, in

a country where rocks were piled upon rocks, and where in some places large masses must be blasted, and in others removed and covered with good soil, before the plow could possibly be employed, required of course a great deal of time and labor; but the industry and zeal with which Oberlin himself began to put in practice every scheme that successively occurred to him, had such an influence upon the minds of his parishioners, that, after the prejudices of the few first years had entirely subsided, they seldom failed to enter into his views, and to imitate his example: the plan was tried, and answered his most sanguine expectations.

In the year 1778, he formed, at the Ban de la Roche, a little Agricultural Society, composed of the more intelligent farmers and the best informed inhabitants of his parish; and, having invited the pastors of the adjacent towns and some of his friends to become members, he connected it with that of Strasbourg, in order to secure the communication of periodical works, and assistance in the distribution of prizes; and the latter Society, wishing to encourage its interesting auxiliary, intrusted to its disposal the sum of two hundred francs, to be distributed among such peasants as should most distinguish themselves in the planting of nursery grounds and in the grafting of fruit-trees.

The good effects resulting from this measure induced Oberlin likewise to form a fund, supported by voluntary contributions, for the distribution of prizes to the farmers of each commune, who should rear the finest ox. A short time afterwards, with a view to prepare the rising generation for continuing the works which their fathers had begun, and to give the opportunity of acquiring useful information, he commenced the plan of devoting two hours every other Thursday morning to a familiar lecture on the subjects of agriculture and of useful science.

Such, indeed, was his assiduity, that not a year rolled away in which some astonishing improvement was not effected in the condition or the morals of his people; and the surrounding districts beheld with admiration the rapid progress that civilization was continually making, in the once neglected and apparently forsaken Steinthal.

CHAPTER IV.

Oberlin's address to his parishioners on the commencement of a new year—Erection of a new school-house in the Ban de la Roche—Progress of civilization—Four other school-houses erected—Introduction of infant schools, under the care of conductrices—Public schools—Weekly assembling of the children at Waldbach, to receive religious instruction—Establishment of a circulating library—Almanac—Christian Society established in 1782—Abrogation of that Society.

While Oberlin was thus zealous in encouraging the progress of agriculture, and in forming his people to habits of industry, he attended with equal solicitude to what related more immediately to his pastoral functions, as the following address to his parishioners, on the commencement of the New Year, 1779, bears ample testimony.

"JANUARY 1, 1779.

"*And he that sat upon the throne said, Behold, I make all things new.*"—Rev. xxi. 5.

"Through the grace of God we have entered upon a new year. O, that it may be new with espect to our sins, our sufferings, and the temptations with which we may have to combat.

"As to sins, may their number diminish day by day, and may we be more constantly animated, and governed, by the spirit of our Lord Jesus Christ. As to sufferings and tribulations, may they produce the effect which God designs in sending them, namely, that of detaching our affections from this transitory world, and of rendering us attentive to his will and Word. May they quicken us to prayer; and induce us to strive more earnestly to enter in at the strait gate, and to 'press toward the mark for the prize of our high calling.' And, as to the temptations which may be placed in our way, may we live entirely to Jesus Christ, and maintain constant communion with him, in order that we may receive, from time to time, fresh supplies of grace and strength to resist them and be enabled to bring forth fruits of right eousness, to the glory of God, and to the hono. of his Holy Gospel. O Lord, be thou pleased with the renewal of the year, to renew ou. strength. O Lord Jesus Christ, thou hast said 'I make all things new.' O make our faith new also.

"May this year be marked by a more lively more deep, and more serious repentance; b greater fervor in supplicating the influences o

God's Holy Spirit; by renewed earnestness in devoting ourselves to Him, and to his service. May we look to Him, and employ all our mental and bodily powers, our time, and our property, to his glory, and to the purpose for which Jesus quitted his throne, namely, the conversion and happiness of mankind. O may we, this year, apply ourselves, with renewed faithfulness, to obey all his commandments, and all his precepts.

"May this year be distinguished by an in crease of the number of the children of God and of the followers of Jesus Christ; by the weakening of the kingdom of Satan within us, and by the coming of the kingdom of God.

"May we, not only during the present, but, also, during each succeeding year which God shall grant us in this probationary world, become more and more prepared for a blessed eternity—abound more in prayers of intercession and supplication—shed more tears of penitence, contrition, love, and pity—and perform more good works, in order that we may reap an abundant harvest on that day, when God, through Jesus Christ, shall 'make all things new.'"

The instruction of *the young* also engaged, in an especial manner, a large portion of Oberlin's care and attention. When he entered on his charge, in 1767, the only regular schoolhouse in the five villages, was Stouber's hut, which, having been constructed of unseasoned wood, was in a most miserable and ruinous condition. His parishioners were, however, very averse to his proposition of erecting a more convenient one; and, instead of feeling grateful for the benefit he intended to confer on their children, complained that, notwithstanding their extreme poverty, he wished to burden them with fresh expenses; alleging, that as the old hut had answered very well hitherto, they were sure it would do for a long time to come. He had no other way of silencing their objections, than by entering into a formal engagement with the overseers of the commune, that neither the expense of building nor repairing the projected school-house, though erected for the public good, should ever become chargeable on the parish funds. Had he not made this stipulation, he would have found in the parents themselves, the most obstinate enemies of his plans for the happiness of their children.

He then applied to some of his benevolent friends at Strasbourg, for assistance in defraying the expenses of the erection. But though the money thus collected, was by no means sufficient for the purpose, and his own little property and narrow income (not exceeding $200) scarcely admitted of his prudently embarking in any undertaking which involved pecuniary responsibility, he resolved to commence it; for neither personal considerations nor the fear of being unable to meet contingent expenses, ever deterred him from putting into execution schemes of usefulness. He had an unbounded confidence in the goodness of his heavenly Father, and was convinced, as he often said, that if he asked for any thing with faith, and it was really right that the thing should take place, it would infallibly be granted to his prayers.—"When, indeed, are our plans more likely to succeed, than when we enter upon them in humble and simple dependence upon God, whose blessing alone can render them successful?"

The event afforded a fresh evidence of this truth. Not only was the projected building completed, without material injury to his own slender finances, but, in the course of a few years, a school-house was erected in each of the other four villages; and, such was the progress of civilization, that the inhabitants came voluntarily forward, and seconded the projects of their pastor, by offering to take upon themselves both the trouble and the expense attending them. During the construction of these necessary buildings the *preparation of masters* continued; but as Oberlin had observed with concern the disadvantages to which the younger children were subjected, whilst their elder brothers and sisters were at school, and their parents busily engaged in their daily avocations, he laid down a plan for the introduction of *infant schools* also; probably the very first ever established, and the model of those subsequently opened at Paris, and still more recently in this country. Observation and experience had convinced him, that, even from the very cradle, children are capable of being taught to distinguish between right and wrong, and of being trained to habits of subordination and industry; and, in conjunction with his wife, he therefore formed *conductrices* for each commune, engaged large ooms for them, and salaried them at his own expense. Instruction, in these schools, was mingled with amusement, and whilst enough of discipline was introduced to instil habits of subjection, a degree of liberty was allowed, which left the infant mind full power of expansion, and information was conveyed which might turn to the most important use in after life. During school hours, the children were collected on forms in great circles. Two women were employed, the one to direct the handicraft, the other to instruct and entertain them. Whilst the children of two or three years old only, were made at intervals to sit quietly by, those of five or six were taught to knit, spin and sew; and, when they were beginning to be weary of this occupation, their conductrice showed them colored pictures relating to Scripture subjects, or natural history, making them recite after her the explanations she gave. She also explained geographical maps of France, Europe, or the Ban de la Roche, and its immediate environs, engraved in wood for the purpose, by Oberlin's direction, and mentioned the names of the different places marked upon them; in addition to this, she taught them to sing moral songs and hymns. Thus she varied their employments as much as possible, taking care to keep them continually occupied, and never permitting them to speak a word of *patois*.*

With minds thus stored and trained by discipline, the children, when arrived at a proper

* By this means correct French was introduced into the Ban de la Roche, and the *patois*, which resembles the old French of the twelfth century, partly abolished.

age, entered what may be called the public schools, and the masters were relieved and encouraged in their duties (which, in such a situation, were sufficiently arduous) by the progress they had already made. Reading, writing, arithmetic, geography, the principles of agriculture, astronomy, and sacred and profane history, were regularly taught in the higher schools; but, although Oberlin carefully superintended the whole proceedings, he reserved for himself, almost exclusively, the *religious* instruction of this large family. Every Sunday the children of each village, in rotation, assembled at the church, to sing the hymns they had learned, to recite the religious lessons which they had committed to memory during the week, and to receive the exhortations or admonitions of their common father.

Besides this Sabbath service, with a view to excite a spirit of emulation between the several schools, and to improve the modes of instruction by comparing those of the several masters, Oberlin established a weekly meeting of all the scholars at Waldbach. This proved a means of stimulating them to industry, for they knew that the "*Cher Papa*," (dear father) as he was designated by all his parishioners, attentively watched their progress, and they were most anxious to secure his approving smiles: so universally was he beloved, that those smiles were regarded by the children, as a sufficient reward for all the labors of the past week.

The success that attended these benevolent, and interesting exertions, inducec his friends at Strasbourg to increase their subscriptions; endowments were even added, (which were lost at the Revolution,) and Oberlin was thus enabled to establish a library of valuable works for the private use of the children; and to have a number of school-books, such as the "Coup d'œil sur la nature," and "L'Ami des Enfans," printed for the exclusive use of the Ban de la Roche; he also made a collection of indigenous plants, and procured an electrical machine, and other philosophical and mathematical instruments. Prizes were likewise awarded to both masters and scholars; and various works upon natural history and other branches of science, some of which he printed at his own expense, put in circulation on the plan of a little book society, being retained for three months at a time, first at one village and then at another, passing successively from house to house, in order that the younger members of the family might be supplied with a continual fund of useful and agreeable information.

Oberlin about this time, drew up an *almanac*, divested of all the falsehoods and superstitions with which those in use were filled, thinking that their tendency was to mislead and deceive uneducated persons. I do not possess a copy of this almanac, but it concludes with the following passages, in reference to the purposes for which it was written, which show that he thought nothing beneath his notice that seemed likely to please or instruct his parishioners.

"*Advice to my countrymen of the Ban de la Roche, upon this Almanac.*

"1. The people of Germany have private almanacs, divided, by means of ruled lines, into a number of partitions. In each partition the names of the different individuals of the family are written, with a little blank space below them, in order that some notice may there be made of the manner in which the day has been past, or any necessary memoranda inserted. I have at length prepared such an almanac for your use.

"2. The Strasbourg children are accustomed to find their baptismal names in their almanac, and to celebrate the days on which they are recorded. You may also do the same with yours. They will all be found in this almanac.

"3. The fathers and mothers of large and numerous families are often puzzled to find pretty baptismal names, to distinguish their children from those who bear the same family name. Henceforth, if they will consult this new almanac, they will soon be enabled to decide.

"4. In your common almanacs you find, and pay for, a number of incomprehensible things; for others absolutely useless; and for others contrary to the commands of God, such as prognostics of the weather, nativities, predictions from the planets according to birth-days, lucky and unlucky days, or good or bad omens. This new almanac is divested of all such nonsense.

"5. The changes of the moon, eclipses, and even some information respecting the course of the planets; the names and figures of the twelve signs of the zodiac; the time of the sun's rising and setting; and even the number of the months, and that of the weeks, are, you will find, nevertheless, inserted here.

"6. I have been frequently asked the signification of names of a strange origin. By means of this almanac, I am enabled to give a reply to all my parishioners, for it contains the signification of every name, which can be ascertained with certainty.

"7. What a pity, you will perhaps say, that it is come so late! I say the same. It ought to have been completed before the end of January. But what good do you possess, the acquisition of which has not been retarded by various delays and obstacles? For my own part, I am so accustomed to expect this, in every thing I do for you, that I am heartily glad it is accomplished, even at this late period.

"8. What does it cost, you will inquire. Dear friends! this almanac is the fruit of my long-cherished desires to promote your good. Accept it as such. If it proves of any real benefit to you, or affords you a moment's gratification, look up to your heavenly Father, and say, 'Thy goodness, O Lord, has crowned me with blessings. Permit me to thank thee for them; and do thou strengthen, by whatever means it may please thee to employ, the feeble faith of thy too feeble child.'"

Oberlin knew how to blend amusement with instruction in the wisest and most judicious manner; and whilst his primary object ever was to ground the young people in the principles of our Christian faith, and to induce them to consider religion as the guardian and inspirer of their happiness, he had also the talent of diffusing amongst them that taste for pastoral and agricultural life, which their circumstances rendered so peculiarly desirable.

In order to familiarize the children of twelve or fifteen years of age with these pursuits, they were accustomed to write, under the direction of their teachers, short essays on agriculture and the management of fruit trees, selected and extracted from the best authors. These they afterwards committed to memory; and, at the annual examination, they were expected to give answers to the questions proposed.

The Ban de la Roche presented a delightful field for botany,* and they were, even at a still earlier period, initiated in the principles of that pleasing science, being allowed to ramble in the woods, in summer, in search of plants, of which they had learned the names and properties during the winter, and to transplant them into little gardens of their own, which their

* Of 4874 species of plants, which compose the French Flora, nearly 700 are found growing naturally in the small extent of uneven surface forming the Haut Champ. The flora of these primitive mountains might be estimated at about 1000, including the *hypoxylons*, and other azotic plants.

The evergreens, such as the lichens, mosses, horse-tails, brakes, hepaticæ, coniferæ, and the families which delight in elevated or umbrageous situations, and little vegetable mould, form the principal clothing of the heights of the Ban de la Roche.—Wilks.

parents had been induced to give them for the exercise of their industry and skill. They were also taught to draw the flowers; an art in which some of them succeeded remarkably well.*

From what has been related, it will be supposed that the schoolmasters were, at this period, persons of a somewhat different description from the shepherd schoolmasters in Stouber's time. Individuals of the first distinction in the village were generally fixed upon for the office, now become a very important one; and indeed at Bellfosse the character of mayor and schoolmaster were at one time united in the same person. They were still called "Régents," according to M. Stouber's original suggestion, and were paid on a plan fixed by law: widows, masters of families and each particular child sent to school, had a certain proportion to pay.

Among other things, the régents were required to impress upon the minds of their pu-

---

* The editor has seen several groups of flowers copied from nature by Oberlin's scholars. She has in her possession a garland of roses and heart's-ease, upon which the children of our charity schools would look with astonishment, were they told it was painted by a poor little boy in similar circumstances with themselves. The following text is neatly written, in French, in the centre:—"Thou shalt also be a crown of glory in the hand of the Lord, and a royal diadem in the hand of thy God."—Isaiah 62: 3. And underneath are inscribed these words:—"Will you, Mr. Legrand, accept this slight token of sincere gratitude, from your humble and dutiful scholar, "GUSTAVUS SCHEIDECKER."

Thus were the little children of the Ban de la Roche accustomed to acknowledge their obligations, to those who kindly took charge of their ed[illegible]ation.

pils, that, from the peculiarity of their local circumstances, (their maintenance depending almost entirely on the products of the valley,) it was a duty incumbent upon the youth to contribute their share towards the general prosperity; and, previously to receiving religious confirmation, they were expected to bring a certificate from their parents, that they had planted, in a spot described, two young trees.*

---

* It is the injunction of the Apostle that "whether we eat, or drink, or whatsoever we do, we do all to the glory of God,"—1 Cor. 10 : 31. The views of religion, which Oberlin entertained, made him bring the greatest principles to the minutest operation. He would take a stone out of the road, if it were likely to incommode a traveller, on the principle of love to his neighbor; and, in this manner, he argued respecting all the duties in which mankind are engaged. Take, for instance, a direction to his people on planting trees. This, with other men, would be an affair of convenience; with him, in his circumstances, it was a religious duty. He thus addressed his parishioners:

"*November* 13, 1803.

"Dear Friends,

"Satan, the enemy of mankind, rejoices when we demolish and destroy. Our Lord Jesus Christ, on the contrary, rejoices when we labor for the public good.

"You all desire to be saved by Him, and hope to become partakers of his glory. Please Him, then, by every possible means, during the remainder of the time you may have to live in this world.

"He is pleased, when, from a principle of love, you plant trees for the *public benefit*. Now is the season. Be willing then to plant them. Plant them also in the best possible manner. Remember you do it to please Him.

"Put all your roads into good condition; ornament them; employ some of your trees for this purpose, and attend to their growth."

The day on which the first fruit was presented to their beloved pastor, was an interesting and useful festival.

Thus were the clouds of ignorance, which had, for a long period, settled on the Ban de la Roche, gradually dispelled by the enlightening influence of Christian education; and this at a time when knowledge was considered unnecessary, and dangerous for the poorer classes; and when the modern systems of cheap and mechanical instruction were almost entirely unknown. The change, that was, in the course of a few years, effected in this place, is the more extraordinary, when we reflect upon the state of the people previous to Oberlin's arrival; and, in contemplating it, we are involuntarily led to unite with him, in ascribing the praise to that great and glorious Being to whom alone it is due, and who had thus caused "the waters to break out in the wilderness, and streams in the desert." The total renunciation of any thing like merit of his own, formed a remarkable and striking feature in Oberlin's character; he regarded himself merely as the *instrument* whom it had pleased God to employ, and was frequently heard to say "I have little merit in the good I have done; I have only that of obedience to the will of God. He has been graciously pleased to manifest his intentions to me, and has always given me the means of executing them."

In the year 1782, Oberlin, in the hope of advancing the spiritual interests of his people established a society, which he denominated "The Christian society." The following is a summary of the Rules, translated from the original, in his own hand-writing.

Rubrics of the Christian Society, for assisting the memory of the Members, and especially that of the Superintendents, whose duty it is to see that they are duly observed.

1. Regeneration.
2. Sanctification.
3. "We are all one in Christ Jesus."
4. "Abide in me."
5. "Christ is all, and in all."
6. "Bring forth much fruit."
7. "Love not the world, neither the things that are in the world."
8. Nourish the inner man, by
   (1.) The word of God.
   (2.) Continual prayer.
   (3.) The frequent use of the Holy Sacrament.
9. The Superintendents are the Overseers, whom the members choose from among themselves.
10. Not only the superintendents, but also all the members, ought to watch over each other for good; to exhort, and to warn each other.
11. With sweetness, charity, humility, and patience.
12. As to the incorrigible—follow the example of Jesus Christ, Matt. 18: 15, 16.
13. Meet for prayer on this subject.

14. Be submissive to your superiors. All the members are fellow-workers with their pastor.

15. Good management.

16. Good education.

17. "Wives, be in subjection to your own husbands."

18. "Search the Scriptures," diligently.

19. Diligence. Diligence with application and energy—that is to say, industry.

20. "Be careful for nothing."

21. Lose no time.

22. Allow of no idleness or negligence, on the part of those confided to your care.

23. Honest and exact payment; no artfulness or cunning.—See Rom. 12: 17.

24. "Be kindly affectioned one to another with brotherly love."

25. Endeavor to promote the happiness of all.

26. "Provoke unto love and to good works."

27. Appropriate part of your earnings, at stated intervals, to the public good."

This Society seems, by the account which is given of it, to have been established for the purpose of *prayer and religious conversation.* It appears to have been violently opposed, and spoken against, by some persons in the parish, which induced Oberlin, in the supposition that the scandal of the bad prevailed over the advantage of the good, to put it down about a year and a half after its formation. At its dissolution, he delivered an address on the subject, to his parishioners. It alludes to the cause of its abrogation; and affords such complete evidence of his devotedness to God, and love to his Savior, as well as boldness in reproving sin and prudence in preventing any just cause of censure, that I give it entire :

May 1, 1783.

"Neither pray I for these alone, but for them also which shall believe on me through their word. That they all may be one; as thou, Father, art in me, and I in thee, that they also may be one in us; that the world may believe that thou hast sent me.—John 17: 20, 21.

"These verses contain the last desire, the last prayer of our gracious Redeemer—his earnest prayer, since it was four times repeated—the union of all his beloved disciples among themselves and with him, as he and the Father are one.

"As the pastor of your parish, a minister of the Gospel, and a servant of Jesus Christ, my aim ought to be to do the will of Jesus Christ; to bring souls to him; and to unite them together in him. Such was my aim, in establishing two years since the Christian Society.

"Every end requires means. I could have wished that all my parishioners might by degrees have associated themselves with it. I have often publicly invited them. Some have complied. More than one hundred and thirty individuals have been friends to it, and have willingly kept company with us, to listen to what was going forward. Some have declared themselves enemies. Some have calumniated it, without even understanding its purport, or wishing to understand it, although the doors of the church were open, and they had, more than two hundred times, the opportunity of remaining to see what passed. Some amongst them, have calumniated it against their conscience. They have said that I placed sentinels at the doors, to prevent those who were not members from entering. This was a downright falsehood.

"By what means then did you come, you from all the five villages—who were so often auditors without being members?

"The greater part of the members did not announce themselves to be such, till they knew and understood the principles, by which the Society was regulated. How were they able to do this, if sentinels were posted to prevent their approach? How did Mr. —— the elder, of Waldbach, and Mr. —— of Foudai, manage, —who, without being members, have been present so frequently? How did Messrs. —— manage?—the family of Marechal, of Waldbach, the founders of Rothau, the wife of M le Régent, and many other persons, who were so often with us, that we were never once alone There have been many other individuals, who were not members, present.

"If they have had the hardihood to invent such falsehoods respecting us, as they now refuse to acknowledge, how much greater may they have invented?

"Your gracious Lord earnestly desires that you should all be true Christians—such as the Gospel portrays—and such as I have endeavored to make you, whether through this Society, or through any other means.

"But, on account of some atrocious calumnies respecting it, I am come to the resolution of abrogating its name and external form:—a thing which I can do the more easily, because Christianity does not consist either in names, or in external forms.

"I abrogate it then to-day; and I abrogate it as fully assured of God's direction in doing so, as I was assured of his direction in its establishment. And this partly for the following reasons:

"1st. I have, in a great measure, obtained the end I had in view.

"2d. Names and external forms are not essential, but are subject to vicissitude.

"3d. In the event of my death or removal, this external form would have been liable to change; and the members, overtaken by surprise, would have resembled, in some degree, sheep without a shepherd, and would not have known what to do. It is better that this should happen during my life-time.

"I have said that I have, in a great measure, obtained my end.

"First. With respect to those who have been willing to become members.

"1st. They have had the opportunity of declaring themselves on the side of their Lord and Savior Jesus Christ, and of acknowledging him, which is a thing of no trivial importance, if we recollect that passage in Matth. 10: 32, 'Whosoever, therefore, shall confess me before men, him will I also confess before my Father which is in heaven.'

"2d. They have learned to know more of their spiritual wants; and how necessary it is for them to be found in Christ Jesus, 'without spot and blameless,' 'rooted and built up in him, and established in the faith.'

"3d. They have felt, more than ever, the duty and necessity of prayer. Many, previous to the formation of this society, had not even an idea of that continual prayer of the heart, which Jesus Christ recommends to his disciples, Luke 18.

"4th. They have been led to feel that many souls are anxious for their salvation. They know, now, where to seek the friends of God, and of Jesus Christ, in order to enjoy the edification and benefit of Christian communion.

"5th. They have learned 'to be kind to one another, tender-hearted, forgiving one another, even as God, for Christ's sake, hath forgiven them.

"Secondly. With respect to those who have not been members. A number of precious souls have been *awakened* from their sleep, and although they could not resolve to declare themselves members, yet they have been induced to pay more attention to their spiritual necessities—have been led to look upon themselves as sinners—have learned to tremble for their salvation—and have become also 'instant in prayer.'

"1st. I cannot sufficiently thank God, the Father of our Lord Jesus Christ, for all the good that he has, through this medium, been pleased to effect in my dear parish; and for the evident blessing that has rested upon it. May he watch over it, and grant that the good fruits brought forth may be perfected, and rendered permanent. May the kingdom of our Lord

Jesus Christ be promoted, and extended, by any other means that he may see meet to appoint.

"2d. May he sustain his church, according to his promise, Mat. 16: 18, so that 'the gates of hell shall not prevail against it.' May He, who said to his disciples, 'He that receiveth you, receiveth me,' register all its members in his Book of Life. May he abundantly shed his Holy Spirit upon them, and 'grave them upon the palms of his hands,' so that no one may be able to draw them away, or to turn them from him. May he protect them, sanctify them, purify them, and prepare them for their heavenly inheritance.

"3d. I thank God also, for all those who have shown themselves friends to this Society. May He reward you for the joy which you have thus imparted to your distressed and afflicted pastor.

"May He bring you nearer and nearer to Jesus. May you become of the number of his own dear people—a people zealous of good works—the sheep of his beloved little flock.

"4th. I thank those who have permitted their wives and children to belong to it, and to declare themselves openly. May God recompense them for all that they have done 'unto the least of my brethren.' May he recompense them also richly and eternally, for the good which they have done to their wives and children, in permitting them to participate in the contempt which Jesus Christ suffered; to bear his cross; and to become partakers in the promıse which our Lord has made to those who confess his name before men.

"O my dear auditors! leave, leave, I entreat you, the ways of Belial. Devote yourselves to the Lord Jesus. He is able and willing to receive every soul that earnestly seeks him; he will cast out none that come unto him; having shed his blood for all, he desires to receive all into his arms. Hasten then to be saved. Time flies away; death draws near. 'There is none other name under heaven given among men whereby we must be saved,' than Jesus Christ, whom I preach unto you. Hasten to him. Fly to him. Pray, mourn, weep; seek after him in the secret of your hearts, until you find him. Amen.

"In the course of the year 1784, Oberlin had the following paper printed in French and German, and placed in a conspicuous station in every cottage throughout his extensive parish. It serves to prove at how early a period the subject of *missions* occupied his mind, and led him to form those *monthly prayer meetings* to promote this object, which are now carried forward by most of the denominations of Christians throughout the world.

"Our Lord Jesus Christ desires his followers to espouse his interests; to aid him in his great work; and to pray in his name. To conduce to this end, he has himself furnished them with one common prayer.

"For the satisfaction and assistance of some individuals amongst us, a sort of Spiritual Association was established a few years ago; and by means of printed sheets, the following articles were agreed upon, and circulated:—

"FIRST. Every member of this Society shall pray, on the first Monday of every month, that the Missionaries employed in the conversion of savage and idolatrous nations in all parts of the world, may be supported and sustained, 'against the wiles of the devil.'

"SECONDLY. Besides habitual 'watching unto prayer,' every individual, if he be able, shall prostrate himself in mind and body, every Sunday and Wednesday, at five o'clock in the evening, to ask of God, in the name of Jesus Christ—

"1st. That every member of this Society may be saved, with *all his household*, and belong to the Lord Jesus Christ.

"2d. Every member shall add to the list, all the friends of God *of his acquaintance*, and pray for them.

"3d. Every member shall include in his prayer all the children of God, *in general*, upon all the earth, of whatever religion they may be, supplicating that they may be united more and more in Christ Jesus.

"4th. Every member shall pray that the kingdom of Satan may be at length destroyed, and that the kingdom of God, and of our Lord Jesus Christ, may be fully and generally established among the innumerable Pagans, Turks, Jews, and nominal Christians.

"5th. Every member shall pray for schoolmasters, superiors, and pious magistrates, of whatever name or rank they may be.

"6th. For faithful pastors, and male and female laborers in the vineyard of the Lord Jesus, who, being themselves devoted to his service, desire, above all things, to bring many other souls to him.

"7th. For the youth, that God may preserve them from the seducing influence of bad example, and lead them to the knowledge of our gracious Redeemer.

"THIRDLY. Every Saturday evening all the members shall ask God to bless the preaching of his Holy Word on the morrow."

CHAPTER V.

Death of Mrs. Oberlin—Its effect upon Oberlin's mind—Louisa Schepler becomes his housekeeper—Letter from the latter—Letter, taken from a German Magazine printed at Tubingen, containing an account of Oberlin and his family, in the year 1793—Death of his eldest son Frederic.*

ANIMATED by desires of usefulness, habitually relying on the goodness of their heavenly Father, and stimulating each other to active exertion in the performance of every Christian

* The editor regrets that she has not been able to procure any particular documents relative to Oberlin's proceedings, in the interval between the death of his wife, in 1784, and that of his son Frederic, in 1793. That his exertions for the good of his flock were, however, carried forward with unrelaxed energy, the improved appearance of the Ban de la Roche, and the extraordinary change effected amongst the young people there, during that period, bear ample testimony. Since writing the above lines, the editor has had the gratification of receiving a corroboration of her statement, from Mr. Heisch. "It was during this period," he writes, "that I mostly visited

duty, Oberlin and his beloved Madeleine passed sixteen years in a union cemented by the ties of the strongest affection. Their family now consisted of seven children, Frederic, Fidelité Caroline, Charles Conservé, Henry Gottfried, Louisa Charité, Henrietta, and Frederica Bienvenue, all of whom were brought up under the paternal roof.*

On the 18th of January, 1784, it pleased God that an event should take place, which had a most powerful influence both upon the cast of his mind and the whole of his future life. This was the loss of his wife. She died rather suddenly, about ten weeks after her last confinement. No unfavorable symptoms, no incipient disease had prepared Oberlin for this distressing separation. When first informed of it, he was so much overpowered as to remain for some moments plunged in the deepest silence, and unable to give utterance to his feelings. At length, after this interval of melan-

---

the Ban de la Roche once a year for a few weeks. I found the different intellectual, religious, and moral engines always at work, with more or less energy; and practical alterations and improvements *always* going forwards."

* "I knew Oberlin," says Mr. Heisch, "as the playfellow and instructor of his children when they were young, and as their *friend* and counsellor when they arrived at years of maturity. In the character of instructor, he so well knew how to mingle affection with earnestness, and even with severity when requisite, that his children both loved and respected him; and in that of a friend, there was an endearing tenderness that not only constituted their happiness, but formed also a constant stimulus to their exertions."

choly stupor, he was observed suddenly to fall on his knees and return thanks to God, that the object of his tenderest solicitude was now beyond the reach or the need of prayer, and that he had crowned the abundance of his mercies towards her, by giving her so easy and gentle a dismissal. He has himself commemorated, in a written fragment, which will be inserted in a future part of this memoir, the emotions by which he was ag tated in these moments of bitter suffering. "Upon this occasion," says he, "as upon a thousand others in the course of my life, notwithstanding my overwhelming affliction, I was upheld, by God's gracious assistance, in a remarkable manner."

From that time the passive graces shone as conspicuously in his character as the active virtues had hitherto done. Neither complaint nor murmur escaped his lips. It might be said that he had not ceased to live in the society of the Christian wife whom he had lost. Every day he devoted whole hours to holding communion with her in those elevated frames of mind, which require not the aid of superstition to make us conscious of the presence of those whom we love. A speedy *reunion*, in the mansions of our Father's house, was, nevertheless, one of his most cherished desires. "I hope," he would often say, "that the world in which God will reunite me to my beloved wife will soon open to me."

This desire had nothing of a transitory character; it was not the mere result of acute grief, nor the effect of any habitual melancholy Although his sorrows might have contributed to strengthen it, it had its origin in a religious feeling. Like St. Paul, he desired to depart to be with Christ, which to him was far better. He longed to be able to unite his voice with hers he had lost, in singing the song of the Lamb, and to participate in that "fullness of joy" which "God hath prepared for those who love him." "I have had all my life," he says, in the paper to which allusion has been already made, and which was written the very year he lost his wife, "a desire, occasionally a very strong one, to die, owing, in some degree, to the consciousness of my moral infirmities, and of my frequent derelictions. My affection for my wife and children, and my attachment to my parish, have sometimes checked this desire, though for short intervals only."

These few words seem to lay open the very secret of his soul. While he was blasting rocks, levelling roads, building bridges, fertilizing fields, improving the morals and promoting the happiness of his flock, the expressions just cited, prove what was the moving principle by which he was actuated. That which induced him to become the benefactor of these districts —that which led him to devote so much time to the prosecution of his plans, was the ever-present thought of death and eternity ; and the habitual remembrance of the responsibility attached to talents, and to opportunities of usefulness. He knew that his soul would be required of him ; he desired that it might be so speedily ; and, in order that he might hear the joyful sound, "Well done, good and faithful servant," he dedicated every faculty he possessed to the interests of others, living himself by faith in the Son of God, and resting entirely on his propitiation.

His patience and resignation not only under this, but under every other affliction that it pleased God to award to him during the whole course of his life, was striking and exemplary. After the first bitterness of grief was over, his soul always seemed "to be girding itself up," and, as it were, "stretching its wings" in expectation of that joyful period when it should leave mortality behind, and soar to the regions of everlasting blessedness—to join "the innumerable company of angels, and the general assembly and church of the first-born." "Millions of times," he continues, in the paper mentioned above, "have I besought God to enable me to surrender myself with *entire* and filial submission to his will, either to live or to die: and to bring me into such a state of resignation, as neither to wish, nor to say, nor to do, nor to undertake any thing, but what He, who only is wise and good, sees to be best."

The following extract from a letter which he wrote to a lady, who had been tried by many successive bereavements, in the hope of convincing her that such dispensations are permitted, to strengthen our graces, and to promote our spiritual refinement, will illustrate his lively faith and fervent piety, as well as the simple and original mode in which he was accustomed to pour out the language of his heart ir epistolary converse. "I have before me two stones, which are in imitation of precious stones. They are both perfectly alike in color;

they are of the same water, clear, pure, and clean; yet there is a marked difference between them, as to their lustre and brilliancy. One has a dazzling brightness, while the other is dull, so that the eye passes over it, and derives no pleasure from the sight. What can be the reason of such a difference? It is this. The one is cut but in a few *facets;* the other has ten times as many. These *facets* are produced by a very violent operation! it is requisite to cut, to smooth, and polish. Had these stones been endued with life, so as to have been capable of feeling what they underwent, the one which has received eighty *facets* would have thought itself very unhappy, and would have envied the fate of the other, which, having received but eight, had undergone but a tenth part of its sufferings. Nevertheless, the operation being over, it is done for ever: the difference between the two stones always remains strongly marked; that which has suffered but little, is entirely eclipsed by the other, which alone is held in estimation, and attracts attention. May not this serve to explain the saying of our Savior, whose words always bear some reference to eternity: 'Blessed are they that mourn, for they shall be comforted.'—Blessed, whether we contemplate them apart, or in comparison with those who have not passed through so many trials. Oh! that we were always able to cast ourselves into his arms, like little children—to draw near to him, like helpless lambs—and ever to ask of him, patience, resignation, an entire surrender to his will, faith, trust, and a heartfelt obedience to the commands which he gives to those who are willing to be his disciples. 'The Lord God will wipe away tears from off all faces.' Isa. 25: 8."

Mrs. Oberlin's death was deeply felt among the poor people of the Ban de la Roche; for although less active and energetic than her husband, she had always evinced the liveliest interest in their concerns, sought to administer to their wants, both secular and spiritual, and to assuage their griefs.

Her loss was in some degree supplied to her own family by a pious orphan, named Louisa Schepler, who had already lived eight years in Oberlin's service, and who now undertook the management of his household and the care of his children.

She was at this time twenty-three years of age; a sensible, pleasing-looking young woman, of mild and gentle manners, habited in the costume of the peasants of the country. She had been a kind of helper in the village of Waldbach, and long one of its most active and zealous *conductrices;* but her health was beginning to be impaired by the severe colds she took in the snows. This circumstance did not, however, lessen her usefulness; and no sooner had she accepted the station of housekeeper to the "dear father," than, refusing offers of marriage, she took the resolution of devoting herself tc his service, and would never accept any salary, but lived in his family rather as a friend than a servant. What her few wants required she asked for—nothing more; and on some occasions, when Oberlin endeavored, through indirect channels, to put money into her hands, she, conjecturing the source from whence it came, uniformly returned it.

The following note, dated "Waldbach, First of the New Year, 1793," addressed by Louisa to her benefactor, is a sweet little proof of her disinterested and grateful affection.

"Dear and beloved Papa,

"Permit me, at the commencement of the new year, to request a favor which I have long desired. As I am now really independent, that is to say, as I have no longer my father nor his debts to attend to, I beseech you, dear papa, not to refuse me the favor of making me your adopted daughter. Do not, I entreat you, give me any more wages; for as you treat me like your child in every other respect, I earnestly wish you to do so in this particular also. Little is needful for the support of my body. My shoes, and stockings, and *sabots*, [wooden shoes,] will cost something, but when I want them I can ask you for them, as a child applies to its father.

"Oh! I entreat you, dear papa, grant me this favor, and condescend to regard me as your most tenderly attached daughter.

"LOUISA SCHEPLER."

The humble request was acceded to, and Louisa was ever afterwards considered as one of Oberlin's own children.

I shall here introduce the following interesting letter, because it presents so lively a picture of the domestic happiness enjoyed under the good pastor's roof at Waldbach, and of the mode of proceeding there, at this period. It is dated March 11th, 1793.

"During the space of nearly thirty years, in which M. Oberlin has been Christian pastor of this canton, he has completely changed it. The language is, from an unintelligible *patois*, altered into pure French; the manners of the people, without degenerating, are civilized; and ignorance is banished without injuring the simplicity of their character. Many of the women belonging to his parishes, trained for the purpose under his paternal care and instruction, (and called *conductrices*,) assist him in his occupations. They teach reading, writing, and the elements of geography, in the different villages where they reside; and through their medium the children are instructed in many necessary things, but, above all, have the seeds of religion and morality sown in their hearts. The excellence of these schools is so well established and appreciated, that girls of the middle ranks are sent to him from distant parts, and the title of a scholar of Pastor Oberlin is no less than a testimonial of piety, cleverness, and gentle manners. His countenance is open, affectionate, and friendly, and bears a strong impress of benevolence. His conversation is easy, flowing, and full of imagination,* yet always adapted to the capacity of those to whom he is speaking. In the evening we accompanied him a league on his

* "Although Oberlin narrated with the vivacity of a painter," says Mr. Heisch, who knew him intimately, "he was extremely strict as to facts, and in all his investigations paid the utmost regard to integrity and truth."

way back to Waldbach. We had a wooded hill to ascend; the sun was just setting, and it was a beautiful evening. 'What sweet thoughts and pious sentiments you have uttered, during this interesting walk,' said M. Oberlin, in a tone of confidence; for he considered us as friends to religion, and servants of God. Our hearts were indeed in unison; and he related to us the circumstances of his past life, and spoke of his views and ideas, and the fear and love of God, in a most touching manner. Sometimes we stood still to admire the beauties of nature, and at others to listen with earnest attention to his impressive discourse. One moment was particularly affecting; when, stopping about half-way up the hill, he answered in the softest tone to our question—'Yes, I *am* happy.' These words are seldom uttered by an inhabitant of this world, and they were so delightful from one who is a stranger to all the favors of fortune—to all the allurements of luxury—and who knows no other joys than those which religion and benevolence impart, that we longed to live like him, that we might also participate in the same happiness.

"The moon rose in all her majesty, and night drew on, before we recollected that the time to return was approaching; when pastor Oberlin exclaimed, 'If five years are necessary to bring a ray of light from Sirius to this world, though travelling at the rate of twelve millions of miles in a minute, how much swifter must the communications of the Spirits be? (Dan. 9: 21.) What is so swift as thought?' and he then imaged to us the facility with which he apprehended we should approach one another in a future state.

"The following morning we set off to return the visit which he had paid us on the preceding day. We found the worthy pastor in his morning gown; it was plain, but whole and clean. He was just on the point of concluding a lecture; his pupils had, like their master, something soft, indeed almost heavenly, in their look.

"The house stands well, and has, from the garden side, a romantic view; in every part of it that kind of *elegance*, which is the result of order and cleanliness, prevails. The furniture is simple; yet it suggests to you that you are in the residence of no ordinary man; the walls are covered with maps, drawings, and vignettes, and texts of Scripture are written over all the doors. That above the dining-room door is, 'Blessed are they which do hunger and thirst after righteousness: for they shall be filled.' And over the others are texts enjoining love to God and our neighbor, The good man implicitly follows the divine command to write them over the door-posts.* On our first entrance, he gave us each, as a welcome, a printed text, 'Abide in me, and I in you,' 'Seek those things which are above,' &c. His study is a peculiar room, and contains rather a well chosen, than numerous, selection of books in French and German, chiefly for youth. The walls are covered with engravings, portraits of eminent characters, plates of insects and animals, and

* See Deut. 6: 6, 7, 8, 9. and 11: 18, 19, 20.

colored drawings of minerals and precious stones; it is, in short, literally papered with useful pictures relative to natural history and other interesting subjects.

"The dinner commenced with a blessing. His children, two maids, and a girl who receives her instruction there, were at the table; there was a remarkable expression of softness in all their countenances.

"Oberlin has a peculiarly happy method of improving occurrences, under the form of similies; and we are mistaken in supposing him a mystic.—'The Gospel,' said he, 'is my standard. I should be afraid of trusting myself alone without it.' He then related to us many of the difficulties he had to encounter, and the sacrifices he had to make, at the commencement of his career in the Ban de la Roche. 'But now,' continued he, checking himself, 'let me observe, it is as great a fault to talk of our own virtues as of the faults of others.'

"It is surprising to witness the sound sense, refinement, and superiority of mind evinced by these simple peasants; the very servants are well educated, and are clothed with that child-like spirit, which is one of the truest tests of real religion. One of them, who is a widow, made many good remarks to us on the duties of married life. 'In order to introduce and preserve domestic peace,' said she, 'let us turn to Him who is peace.'

"I am writing this at his table, whilst he is busy preparing leather gloves for his peasant children. His family are around him, engaged in their different avocations; his eldest son,

Frederic, is giving a lesson to some of the little ones, in which amusement and instruction are judiciously blended; and the dear father, without desisting from his employment, frequently puts in a word. He took me this morning into his work-shop, where there is a turner's lathe, a press, a complete set of carpenter's tools, also a printing-press, and one for book-binding. I assisted him in coloring a quire of paper, which is intended for covers of school-books. He gives scarcely any thing to his people but what has been, in some measure, prepared by his own or his children's hands.

"He will *never* leave this place. A much better living was once offered to him—'No,' said he, 'I have been ten years learning every head in my parish, and obtaining an inventory of their moral, intellectual, and domestic wants; I have laid my plan. I must have ten years to carry it into execution, and the ten following to correct their faults and vices.'

"Pastor Oberlin is too modest and generous not to bear testimony to the worth of his predecessor, who had begun to clear this wilderness, and to raise the superstructure, which he has so beautifully completed.

"Yesterday, I found him encircled by four or five families who had been burnt out of their houses; he was dividing amongst them articles of clothing, meat, assignats, books, knives, thimbles, and colored pictures for the children, whom he placed in a row according to their ages, and then left them to take what they preferred. The most perfect *equality* reigns in his house;—children, servants, boarders,—are al treated alike; their places at table change, that each in turn may sit next to him, with the exception of Louisa, his housekeeper, who of course presides, and has two maids, who sit at the bottom of the table. As it is his custom to salute every member of his family, night and morning, these two little maids come very respectfully curtsying to him, and he always gives them his hand and inquires after their health, or wishes them good night. All are happy, and appear to owe much of their happiness to him. They seem to be ready to sacrifice their lives to save his. The following reply was made by one of his domestics, on his questioning her about her downcast looks during some trivial indisposition: 'I fear, dear papa, there will be no servants in heaven, and that I shall lose the happiness of waiting upon you.'

"Oberlin appears to be looking forward to his eternal home with holy confidence and joyful hope."

The following are specimens of the texts referred to in the preceding letter. They were *printed* by Oberlin himself. He always kept a large supply of them, and distributed thousands and tens of thousands of them to his friends and visitors, often writing a few appropriate words on the back of the paper, or some short sentence expressive of his affectionate remembrance.

My mother and my brethren
are these
which hear the word of God,
and do it.
Luke 8: 21.

And let us
consider one another,
To provoke unto love and to
good works.
Hebrews 10 : 24.

Sometimes, instead of a text a few verses were inscribed on the cards.

My God! to obtain happiness!
Thou hast put me upon earth.
Thou knowest better than I,
What my true wants are:
The heart of thy child
Gives itself back to thy care;
Give me those virtues
Which will enable me to please thee.

Oberlin's house was, as the writer of the preceding letter remarks, literally papered with pictures, inscriptions, verses from the Bible, and directions for missionary and other prayers; and on the door of one of them the Moravian text-book was fastened. The inscription placed on that of another will give some idea of the cordial and warm reception with which he always greeted his visitors, and formed, indeed, throughout, the law by which they were governed:—

"Constant goodness.
Steady sweetness.
Vigorous and unalterable charity."

Towards the latter end of the year 1793, Oberlin's eldest son Frederic, to whom he was most tenderly attached, entered the army as a volunteer, and was one of the first who were killed, being at this time in the twenty-fourth year of his age.

His father's patient resignation, and submission to the will of God, shone forth in as remarkable a manner on this afflicting occasion as they had done on the death of his wife.

"I went soon afterwards," writes Mr. Heisch "to Waldbach, and naturally expected to find a tinge of melancholy spread over the family at the parsonage; but instead of that, I observed only an air of quiet seriousness, and the usual tone of reciprocal communication was uninterrupted among them. They spoke of Frederic not as of the dead, but as one *gone before* them to heaven, where they confidently hoped, sooner or later, to meet him again. Every thing proceeded as usual, except in rather a more serious manner, whilst they thus conversed about him, and it was evident to all around them that they placed the most unlimited confidence in God's unerring goodness."

The firm belief that every event of our lives is under the guidance and direction of a superintending Providence, and that Infinite Wisdom can, from a variety of dispensations, produce a uniformity of good and an uninterrupted series of benefits, formed, indeed, a leading trait in Oberlin's character; in proportion as he suffered under affliction, his mind seemed to open to the consolations of faith; and it is not surprising that the influence and *example* of one so much beloved and respected, should induce other individuals, and especially those of his domestic circle, to adopt the same sentiments, to utter the same language, and to act upon the same principles.—Happy are those who can thus trace the hand of God in every circumstance, prosperous or adverse—who can regard even the heaviest trials as an intended means of sanctification, and of drawing us nearer to Jesus:—and hence, learning to "glory in tribulation," can anticipate with joyful hope that period "when sorrow and sighing shall flee away."

CHAPTER VI.

Unmolested state of the Ban de la Roche during the period of the Revolution—Oberlin's generous renunciation of his own interests for the sake of his parishioners—His school for the children of foreigners—His sentiments respecting the payment of tithes—Letter containing a plan for their disbursement—Purchase of assignats—His influence in exciting a spirit of Christian charity among his people—Account of Sophia Bernard, &c.—Oberlin becomes a correspondent of the British and Foreign Bible Society—Letters addressed by him to members of the London committee—Mode of collecting subscriptions and donations for charitable purposes, in the Ban de la Roche—Letter to his scholars.

During the period of the Revolution, which was at this time agitating the country, and plunging the people into misery and distress, Oberlin was, like the rest of the clergy, deprived of his scanty income. Soon after its commencement, indeed, it had been agreed by the heads of the parish that a *collection* of 1400 francs should be made for him, by persons going about from house to house for the purpose; but although their benevolent efforts were exerted to the utmost, they could not raise, during the year 1789, more than 1133 francs, and in the following one not so many as 400. This sum therefore, for two successive years, constituted nearly his sole revenue; for no fees were admitted. "My people," he used to say, "are born, married, and buried, free of expense, at least as far as their clergyman is concerned."

At length the "reign of terror," which had for the last four years been preparing, by the gradual breaking down of every religious and social tie, raged in all its horror—spreading, like the sirocco of the desert, devastation, famine and dismay. The Ban de la Roche *alone*, seemed to be an asylum of peace in the midst of war and carnage. Though every kind of worship was interdicted throughout France, and almost all the clergy of Alsace, men of learning, (among whom was his elder brother, Professor Oberlin,) talents and property were imprisoned—Pastor Oberlin was allowed to continue his work of benevolence and instruction unmolested.* His house, in fact, became the

* Once, indeed, in the year 1789, he was cited before the Supreme Council of Alsace, and had to clear himself from the accusation of having induced his parishioners to enrol themselves under the banners of Joseph the Second. He was not merely acquitted, but the court, informed by means of this proceeding of his virtues, and of the good that he had effected, after pronouncing judgment in his favor, expressed regret that so estimable an individual should have been drawn from his solitude, to the interruption of the exercise of his charitable labors.

retreat of many individuals of different religious persuasions, and of distinguished rank, who fled thither under the influence of terror, from Strasbourg and its environs, and who always received the most open-hearted and cordial reception, though it endangered his own situation. "I once," says a gentleman, who was then residing at Waldbach, "saw a chief actor of the Revolution in Oberlin's house, and in that atmosphere he seemed to have lost his sanguinary disposition, and to have exchanged the fierceness of the tiger for the gentleness of the lamb."

It is pleasing to see how a Christian minister could meet the difficulties of times like these, and how one of Oberlin's courage and aptitude could make the circumstances of so alarming a period, bend to his aim of profiting those committed to his charge. I will here insert a paper which he addressed to the younger members of his flock, in 1794, and wherein he took advantage of the actual state of the government to teach them what true republicans should really be:

"Young people are precious in the sight of God and of good men, when they are truly what they ought to be,—noble-minded, courageous, diligent, modest, pious, humble, docile, willing to employ all their energies for the welfare of their families, full of respect towards their superiors, and desirous of keeping the commandments.

"I desire that the numerous members of the French Republic should be animated by truly republican sentiments. I wish them to understand that public happiness const .utes private happiness, and that every individual ought therefore to endeavor to live for the public good; and to remember that his actions will only secure the favor and love of God, according to the motives from which they are performed.

"We are Republicans, when we neither live, nor act, nor undertake any thing, nor choose a profession or situation, nor settle in life, except for the public good.

"We are Republicans, when from love to the public we endeavor, by precept as well as by example, to stimulate our children to active beneficence; and seek to render them useful to others, by turning their attention to such pursuits as are likely to increase the public prosperity.

"We are Republicans, when we endeavor to imbue the minds of our children with the love of science, and with such knowledge as may be likely, in maturer life, to make them useful in the stations they are called to occupy; and when we teach them to 'love their neighbors as themselves.'

"Lastly, we are Republicans, when we preserve our children from that self-interested spirit, which, at the present day, seems to have gained more ascendency than ever over a nation whose people have, notwithstanding, sworn to regard each other, and to love each other as brethren, but the greater part of whom care only for themselves, and labor only for the public good when they are compelled to do so

Ah! far from us be this infernal spirit, as anti-republican as it is anti-christian.

"Oh, may you, my young friends, be counted henceforth among the active benefactors of your country.

"Oh, may you render yourselves worthy of this honorable title, by endeavoring to devote to the public good, and to the general happiness, your strength, your abilities, your leisure, and your talents; and by dedicating to this purpose all your attainments in knowledge, philosophy, and science.

"You will then become precious in the sight of all good men, and God will protect and love you, and cause your undertakings to prosper. He will also one day recompense your faithfulness, by loading you with honor, and glory, and power, and riches, and happiness, and by saying to you, in the presence of the assembled universe, 'Well done, good and faithful servant; thou hast been faithful over a few things, I will make thee ruler over many things: enter thou into the joy of thy Lord. Matt. 25: 23. O God, grant that the Republic, and all true republicans, may prosper. Amen."

Upon the re-opening of the churches, in 1795, that benevolent renunciation of his own interests for the good of his flock, which, as I have frequently had occasion to observe, formed so distinguished a feature in Oberlin's character, was strikingly displayed; for he declared that in consequence of their reduced means he was willing henceforth, as long as God should grant him strength to do so, to serve them without any given salary, and that he wanted no annual collections; adding, that as every one knew how to find his way to the parsonage, he *might bring* his share, to whatever amount, and at whatever time he pleased; for he considered it unjust that the poor, who were at times unable to procure either salt or bread, and who formed the greater part of the community, should pay as much as those who were in more affluent circumstances. Nor had they, he assured them, any reason to fear his displeasure, even if they brought nothing at all, since he should consider that it was only for want of ability to do so; and it always afforded him more gratification to relieve than to oppress them. With respect to the payment of the schoolmasters also, they were to adopt the same plan, that is, to contribute according to their means, and to bring whatever they could afford, either for this, or other charitable purposes, to him, in the form of goods, provisions, or cash. This they regularly did; and his faithful Louisa was accustomed to assist him in the judicious distribution of the articles or money thus collected.* In return for these gifts, he always presented the donors with a few words of acknowledgment on the back of one of the papers on which his texts were printed, and of which

* "In spite of the smallness of his resources, he knew how to make them sufficient for every thing; and had by his example, made his parishioners contract the precious habit of putting aside, each week, a portion of their savings for pious purposes; and by this means, they found themselves in a state to encourage, and assist in sustaining, many of the institutions established in the true spirit of the gospel."

specimens have been given. He always kept the most *strict account* of every expenditure, and was never known to *owe* even so much as a single sou to any person. One of the maxims which, among many others, he used to endeavor to impress upon the minds of his people, was that they "ought to avoid debts as they would do the evil spirit."

Notwithstanding the poverty of its inhabitants, scarcely a mendicant was ever seen in the valley, unless indeed some pauper from the neighboring communes, attracted by the well-known disposition of the pastor and his people, might have wandered thither to implore that assistance which, if deserving, he never failed to receive. "Why do you not work?" was Oberlin's usual interrogation. "Because no one will employ me," was the general reply. "Well then, I will employ you. There—carry these planks—break those stones—fill that bucket with water—and I will repay you for your trouble."

Such was his usual mode of proceeding; and idle beggars were taught to come there no more.

But how, it will naturally be asked, were Oberlin and his family supported, and even enabled to assist others, when deprived not only of their little income, but also of the annual contributions of their parishioners?

It appears, indeed, to have been owing to the extraordinary interposition of Providence, that they were watched over and cared for in so peculiar a manner, at a time when many individuals were reduced to the most forlorn situation, and compelled to forsake their home and their country. The gospel reduces to very little the sufficiency of the Christian; and as, in the days of greater prosperity, they had accustomed themselves to habits of the strictest economy and the most rigorous self-denial, in order to facilitate their power of assisting others, so now, in the season of adversity, God did "not leave them comfortless," but supplied all their necessary wants, and supported, strengthened, and blessed them. The principal circumstance that gave Oberlin any uneasiness, was the diminution in his means of doing good; and in the year 1794, with the hope of increasing it, he announced his intention of undertaking the charge of ten or twelve *pupils* whose education should devolve almost entirely upon himself, although he had to provide for his own family of six children, the youngest of whom was now ten years of age, and to superintend their instruction.

The children of several foreigners of distinction were soon committed to his charge; and, in the true spirit of philanthropy, he appropriated a considerable part of the emoluments which he received for their education to the improvements and institutions of his parish.

The duty of devoting a certain portion of his property to charitable purposes, was a subject that had weighed heavily on his mind for some years previous to the Revolution. He had happened to read one day, with more attention than usual, the accounts of the tithes in the Books of Moses, and had been so struck with some of them as to resolve from that moment to devote *three tithes* of all he possessed to the service of God and the poor. The resolution was no sooner made than put into execution, for whatever Oberlin conceived it to be his duty to do, he conscientiously, and without delay, set about it. From that period till the end of his life, even during the most calamitous seasons of the Revolution, he always scrupulously adhered to the plan, and often said that he "*abounded in wealth.*"

The following letter contains an account of the passages that struck him so particularly, and of the manner in which he set about the dedication of the tenths.

"My dear friend,

"You ask me for some explanation respecting the different tithes which God has commanded us to pay. I will tell you how I manage. I endeavor to devote three tithes of all that I earn, of all that I receive, and of all my revenue, of whatever name or nature it may be, to his service, or to useful objects.

"For this purpose I keep three boxes; the first for the first tithe; the second for the second; and the third box for the third tithe.

"When I cannot pay ready money all at once, I mark how much I owe upon a bit of paper, which I put into the box; and when, on the contrary, a demand occurs which ought to be defrayed by one of the three allotments, and there is not sufficient money deposited, I advance the sum, and make the box my debtor by marking upon it how much it owes me

"By this means I am always able to assist in any public or charitable undertaking; and as God has himself declared that 'it is more blessed to give than to receive,' I look upon this regular disbursement of part of my property rather in the light of a privilege than a burden.

"*The first of the afore-mentioned boxes contains a deposit for the worship of God.*

"I put a paper, with the following verses from the Old Testament written upon it, into this box:—

"And all the tithe of the land, whether of the seed of the land, or of the fruit of the tree, is the Lord's: it is holy unto the Lord.—Lev. 27: 30.

"Bring ye all the tithes into the storehouse, that there may be meat in mine house, and prove me now herewith, saith the Lord of hosts, if I will not open you the windows of heaven, and pour you out a blessing, that there shall not be room enough to receive it.—Mal. 3: 10.

"I devote the contents of this box to the building and repairing of churches and school-rooms; the support of conductrices, and the purchase of Bibles and pious books; in short, to any thing connected with divine worship, or the extension of the knowledge of our Redeemer's kingdom.

"My parishioners are at liberty to recall from this tithe any present that either generosity, or the supposition that I expected it, may have induced them to make me.

"*The second box contains tithes for useful purposes.*

"I have written the following passages in it:

"Thou shalt truly tithe all the increase of thy seed, that the field bringeth forth year by year. And thou shalt eat before the Lord thy God, in the place which he shall choose to place his name there, the tithe of thy corn, of thy wine, and of thine oil, and the firstlings of thy herds and of thy flocks; that thou mayest learn to fear the Lord thy God always. And if the way be too long for thee, so that thou art not able to carry it; or if the place be too far from thee, which the Lord thy God shall choose to set his name there, when the Lord thy God hath blessed thee: then shalt thou turn it into money, and bind up the money in thine hand, and shalt go unto the place which the Lord thy God shall choose: and thou shalt bestow that money for whatsoever thy soul lusteth after, for oxen, or for sheep, for wine, or for strong drink, or for whatsoever thy soul desireth: and thou shalt eat there before the Lord thy God, and thou shalt rejoice, thou and thine household, and the Levite that is within thy gates; thou shalt not forsake him; for he hath no part nor inheritance with thee.—Deut. 14: 22—27.

"Three times in a year shall all thy males appear before the Lord thy God in the place which he shall choose; in the feast of unleavened bread, and in the feast of weeks, and in the feast of tabernacles: and they shall not appear before the Lord empty.—Deut. 16: 16.

"I employ this tithe for a variety of purposes:—

"1. For the improvement of the roads to the churches and schools.

"2. For the schoolmasters' salaries.

"3. For all works of public utility.

"4. For the little expenses incurred by my becoming godfather.

"5. For Sunday dinners to my poor people

of the other villages. [*My parishioners might add to this catalogue.*]

"6. For the churchwardens. [*For whether they do their duty voluntarily from love to God or make a claim upon me, I always pay them well.*]

"7. For expenses incurred among the peasantry of Belmont, Foudai, and Zolbach.

"8. For what the poor of Waldbach spend, by inviting the poor of the other villages to come and see them.

"9. For the repairing of injuries.

"*The third box contains tithes for the poor.* [That is, it contains the third tithe every three years, or the thirtieth every year.]

"I have written there the following texts:—

"At the end of three years thou shalt bring forth all the tithe of thine increase the same year, and shalt lay it up within thy gates. And the Levite (because he hath no part nor inheritance with thee), and the stranger, and the fatherless, and the widow, which are within thy gates, shall come, and shall eat and be satisfied; that the Lord thy God may bless thee in all the work of thine hand which thou doest.—Deut. 14: 28, 29.

"And when you reap the harvest of your land, thou shalt not wholly reap the corners of thy field, neither shalt thou gather the gleanings of thy harvest. And thou shalt not glean thy vineyard, neither shalt thou gather every grape of thy vineyard: thou shalt leave them for the poor and stranger: I am the Lord your God —Levit. 19: 9, 10.

"I devote the contents of this box to the service of the poor; to the compensation of losses occasioned by fire;* to wood, flannel,

* Oberlin one year devoted part of the contents of this box to the purchase of a large *fire-engine*, as well as of a

and bread, for those who stand in need, &c. &c."

It must not be supposed from this statement that Oberlin's benevolence was, however, confined to the Ban de la Roche, for the knowledge of several pious and excellent institutions had reached the secluded valley before it spread to the rest of France. One of the first that attracted his attention, as I have observed in a previous chapter, was the Missionary Society. No sooner had he learned that there were pious Christians who left their homes to convey to the benighted heathen the promises of the Gospel, than he parted with all his *plate*, with the exception of one silver spoon,* and contributed the proceeds of the sale to that noble undertaking, as he rightly designated it, only regretting that he was unable to send more.

He was indeed himself actuated by the genuine missionary spirit; and in the early part of his ministry, he for some time hesitated whether he should not accept an invitation to undertake a station in Pennsylvania. For two years a pastor had in vain been sought to fill the vacant post. When informed of this circumstance, Oberlin, considering it to be the duty of a minister of Christ to repair whither others were unable to go, and thinking that the Ban de la Roche might be more easily provided for, than so distant a charge, expressed his readiness to set off. His wife participated

small one that could be easily transported to the mountainous districts.

* Oberlin bequeathed this silver spoon to the Missionary Institution at Basle.

in his sentiments, but, whilst they were waiting for more specific directions, the war broke out between England and America, and prevented their departure. From that time he rejected every station that offered, showing himself to be proof against repeated and urgent solicitations. "Some persons," said he one day, "think it a merit in me to have refused more considerable cures than this; but you," continued he, addressing himself to a military gentleman, who had been expressing his surprise that he had not accepted the charge of larger parishes, "if your general had given you a post to defend, would you quit it without positive orders?" On being answered in the negative—"Well," said he, "God has confided this flock to my care; and why should I abandon it? Where could I find better parishioners, or more grateful hearts?"

His imagination had been powerfully affected also by a description of the wretched condition of the negro slaves in the West Indies, employed in the cultivation of sugar and coffee, which induced him to form the resolution of never again *tasting* either the one or the other, a resolution to which he strictly adhered, although, having been accustomed to them from his earliest infancy, it cost him some little self denial to submit to the deprivation.

Another proof of Oberlin's benevolence, an perhaps a more extraordinary one, considering his very narrow resources, than any that has yet been adduced, was the point he made of buying up assignats, (the paper-money of the Revolution which was never redeemed,) whenever they were introduced into the Ban de la Roche.

"His fidelity in great and little things indiscriminately," says Mr. Legrand in a letter to Mr. Heisch, "was so scrupulous, that he would have believed it displeasing to God, in the remembrance of whose presence he habitually lived, to have written a word, or even a single letter without care. He thought it his duty to give every letter its due honor.

"When the assignats lost their value, he feared that this would bring a curse upon France, and diminish the confidence that the people ought to have in the government.* Convinced that it behooved every individual to use his utmost endeavors, as far as his influence or means extended, to prevent such a calamity, (leaving it to God to bless the example,) he made a public sale every year of agricultural implements and other useful articles amongst

* "The Directory, which succeeded the convention of 1794, tried to renew the system of paper-money in France in the shape of territorial notes (mandats territoriaux), by means of which it was intended to withdraw the assignats from circulation at the rate of thirty for one, and they were to circulate as money. An issue of territorial notes to the amount of 2,400,000,000 of francs, was decreed by the councils. They possessed this advantage, that they might be changed immediately on presentation for the national domains which they represented, and a great portion of which were by this means sold. In this manner was completed the revolutionary cycle of assignats, of which they formed the second period. They procured the Directory a momentary supply, but they in turn also lost their credit, and insensibly led the way to bankruptcy, which was the transition from paper to cash payments."—*Mignet's History of the French Revolution.*

his parishioners, or rather offered them in ex change for assignats. By this means he managed to redeem, in the space of twenty-five years, all the ass'gnats of the Ban de la Roche, and of some of its environs.

"Thus the formation of a single letter was not too small an object to claim the attentio of this true servant of God; nor the redemp tion of thousands of assignats too great an object to be conceived and begun by the poor pastor of the Ban de la Roche."

I possess one of these assignats purchased by Oberlin. It is dated Waldbach, May 9, 1798, and has this superscription upon it in his own handwriting.

"Thus thanks to God, my nation is again discharged in an honest manner of this obligation of 125 francs."

He gave texts of scripture, as a receipt for the assignats, and generally wrote on the back of the card: "Assignat of —— received of M. the minister O." with the date.

Such extreme devotedness to the interests of his flock, combined with his peculiarly endearing and *affectionate manners*, necessarily caused Oberlin to be loved and revered as a father. Every lip became eloquent in his praise—every voice pronounced his name with grateful benedictions—and the stranger wh visited the pine-covered hills and verdant vale of the once wild and forsaken Ban de la Roche, found there in the place of a set of rude and ignorant savages, an industrious, decent, orderly, and well-informed peasantry, many of whom had been so far initiated into both the doctrines and the spirit of the New Testament, as to live in the constant exercise of that love which is said to be the "fulfilling of the law,' and which the Apostle inculcates as a necessary mark of true religion when he says, "He who loveth God must love his brother also."

The exemplary conduct and sincere piety of ome of these individuals, indeed, proved that they had not received "the grace of God in vain." Among other fruits of faith, their *charity to orphans* was particularly striking. When a poor father or mother died, leaving a numerous family, it was a thing of course for some poor person to offer to take upon himself the charge and care of the orphans; so that many of the households contained one or two of these adopted children, and they seldom thought of mentioning that they were not their own.

Three individuals more particularly noted in the annals of the Ban de la Roche for their disinterested benevolence, were Sophia Bernard and Catherine Scheidecker, of Foudai, and Maria Schepler of the hamlet La Hutte, near Belmont, whose names will appear again in a subsequent part of this memoir.

The former, Sophia Bernard, although depending for subsistence on her own labor and he scanty produce of a morsel of land, reolved in early life to devote herself entirely to the care of orphans, and with this view collected, first under her father's roof and afterwards in the old parsonage, several children, whose parents were of different denominations, and taught them t\) spin cotton in order to assist in their maintenance, which would other wise have devolved entirely on herself. Before she married, and when her little family already consisted of seven children, she and her sister Madeleine* received a letter from a poor tailor, named Thomas, who lived in the neigh boring Roman Catholic village, entreating them from what he had heard of their charitabl deeds, to take charge of his three little children, all of whom were under four years old, as his wife was near her confinement, and he was utterly unable to provide for them.

Following the benevolent impulse of the moment, or rather the dictates of that benevolence by which they were habitually actuated, the two sisters immediately set out, although the evening was already far advanced, and they had dangerous roads to traverse, with their baskets on their backs. At length, regardless of fatigue and exertion, they reached the summit of the mountain upon which Thomas's cottage was situated. Softly approaching it, they peeped in at the window, and were confirmed in the truth of the statement they had received, by the evident marks of wretchedness and poverty that the little apartment exhibited. Upon entering it, they found the little creatures in as forlorn a condition as the poor man had described, miserably nursed, and weak and dis eased from neglect. They, therefore, withou farther deliberation, wrapped them up in flannel, packed them in the baskets at their backs,

* Now Madeleine Bernard the regent of Belmont's wife, and a truly exemplary character. She and Sophia married two brothers.

and trudged home with them. But, as their father's house would not accommodate so large an accession to the family, Sophia hired a servant girl, and an additional room, where she fed, clothed, nourished and educated them, so hat they became strong, healthy and industrius. On some of his neighbors afterwards asking the tailor how he could allow his children to be brought up by *Protestants*,—"Oh," he replied, "if they make such good Protestants of them as they are themselves, I shall thank them for it."

Such are the delightful fruits of genuine Christian benevolence! and how strikingly does this fact speak for the admonition of many in another rank of life from that in which these poor women shone so brightly!

While the good effects of Oberlin's instructions and example were thus shedding their benign influence upon the more immediate scene of his pastoral labors, his name and zeal became known in England; and in the year 1804, on the first establishment of the British and Foreign Bible Society in this country, it was judged expedient to open a correspondence with him, for the sake of forming a central point for the distribution of Bibles in France.

Being firmly assured that the Scriptures are indeed "the power of God unto salvation to every one that believeth," he had long and ardently desired their general circulation. He therefore gladly hailed the proposition, and became the *first foreign* correspondent of that Society. The large principle on which this Institution was established, admirably suited the mind of Oberlin, and having for the course of twenty years prayed expressly for Missionaries, as well as for a still longer period, "Thy kingdom come," it would have been extremely unnatural if he had not supported a Society, whose express object it is to open channels fo conveying the streams of the "waters of life' to those parched and desolate portions of th earth which they have not yet pervaded, and to hold out the invitation—"Ho, every one that thirsteth, come ye to the waters."

In conjunction with his youngest son, Henry Gottfried,* a young man of truly eminent piety and much evangelical zeal, Oberlin, under the direction of the London Committee, shortly afterwards organized a little society at Waldbach; and, through its medium, depositories were established in different parts of France, and more than *ten thousand* copies of the New Testament put in circulation. This was some years before the Paris Bible Society was instituted. The Ban de la Roche became also in a manner the cradle of Ladies' Bible Associations, in consequence of a letter addressed by the late venerable pastor to the Committee of the Parent Society, in which he made mention of the three humble but admirable women, whose names, and especially that of Sophia

* The author of the Propositions Geologiques, &c. referred to in a preceding note. He took the degree of Doctor in Medicine at Strasbourg in 1806, and was afterwards ordained. At the time the Archives du Christianisme were announced, he had formed the plan of a religious magazine, and prepared the prospectus of the work.

Bernard, have already appeared in this chapter as suitable persons for taking an active part in this work of love, either by reading the Bible to their neighbors, or by adopting the simple and ingenious plan of lending them the Sacred Volume. The Rev. John Owen, in his History of the British and Foreign Bible Society, adverts to this circumstance, acknowledging the obligations we are under to that extraordinary man, whom he describes as "uniting the simplicity of a patriarch with the zeal of an Apostle."

The letter referred to, is so interesting that no apology appears necessary for inserting it. It is dated, Waldbach, Nov. 3, 1804.

"Accept, my dearest friend, our most unfeigned thanks for the sum of £30, which you have transmitted to us as a kind present from some English friends, for the purpose of purchasing French and German Bibles to distribute among the poor inhabitants of the Ban de la Roche and its neighboring villages, in which there are people of four different religious denominations, namely, Roman Catholic, Lutherans, Reformed, and Anabaptists. May God, for Christ's sake, impart his blessing to this act of Christian benevolence, in order that his name may be glorified, and his kingdom come.

"You will be glad to learn some particulars respecting the use which I intend to make of this money.

"I have ordered, and expect soon to receive, fifty copies of the French Protestant Bible printed at Basle. Though the type is rather too small for country people, yet we have great reasoı to bless God for having enabled us to procure even these. In the mean time, I have made a list of such persons as I consider most deserving of so valuable a present. Among the large number of individuals and families to whom a Bible is a most welcome gift, I first put down such characters as are most active in promoting the coming of the Redeemer's kingdom, and in doing good to the bodies and souls of their fellow-creatures.

"1. The *first* Bible shall be given as a present to Sophia Bernard, who is one of the most excellent women I know, and, indeed, an ornament to my parish. While unmarried, she undertook, with the consent of her parents, the support and education of three helpless boys, whom their inhuman father had often trampled under his feet, and treated in a manner too shocking to relate, when, nearly starving with hunger, they ventured to cry out for food. Soon afterwards she proved the happy means of saving the lives of three Roman Catholic children, who, without her assistance, would have fallen a prey to want and famine. Thus she had the management of six children, to whom several more were added, belonging to parents of three several denominations. She then hired a house and a servant girl, and supported the whole of the family entirely by her own work and the little money acquired by the industry of the children, whom she taught to spin cotton. At the same time she proved the greatest blessing to the whole village where she lived; for it would be impossible for any one to be more industrious, frugal, clean, cheerful, and edifying by her whole walk and conversation more ready for every good word and work; more mild and affectionate, and more firm and resolute in dangers, than she was. Satan once so enraged some of her enemies, that they threatened to destroy her old tottering cottage, but God was graciously pleased to preserve her. A fine youth, of a generous disposition, made her an offer of marriage, and as she appeared unwilling to accept him, he declared that if necessary he would wait ten years to gain her hand. She then acknowledged that her motive for refusing him was the grief it would occasion her to part from her little orphans. "He who takes the mother takes the children also," replied the young man. On this condition the marriage took place, and all the children were brought up under their mutual care in the most excellent manner. They have lately taken in some other orphans, whom they are training up in the fear and love of God. Though these excellent people pass for rather rich, yet their income is so limited, and their benevolence so extensive, that they sometimes hardly know how to furnish themselves with a new suit of necessary clothes. I intend to give *them* a Bible because their own is very often lent out in different Roman Catholic villages.

"2. A *second* Bible I intend to give to an excellent woman, named Maria Schepler, who lives at the opposite end of my extensive parish, where the cold is more severe, and the ground unfruitful, so that nearly all the householders are poor people, who must *lend* their clothes to each other when they intend to go to the Lord's supper. This poor woman is also a very remarkable character; and I could say much in her praise were I to enter into particulars. Though distressed and afflicted in her own person and circumstances, yet she is a mother, benefactress, and teacher, to the whole village in which she lives, and to some neighboring districts too. She takes the most lively interest in all that relates to the Redeemer's kingdom upon earth, and often groans under a sense of the grievous inroads made by the powers of darkness. She, also, has brought up several orphans without receiving the smallest recompense; keeps a free-school for females, and makes it a practice to lend her Bible to such as are entirely deprived of it.

"3. A *third* Bible present I intend to make to an excellent widow woman, Catharine Scheidecker, who is, like the former, a mother to orphans, and keeps a free-school; so also does another young woman, who instructs little children, in a neighboring village, in such knowledge as may render them useful members of society.*

"I might easily enumerate many more characters of a similar description, whose eyes will overflow with grateful tears, if they are favored with the present of a Bible. I will make one observation as to the Bibles which you may send us. It is necessary in our parts, to have a number of copies in readiness *to lend out* to

* Catharine Banzet, who voluntarily attended to all the knitting schools.

the people of the neighboring districts, most of whom are Roman Catholics; for if they possess a Bible of their own, they are in danger of having it taken by some blind Popish priests; whereas if it is only lent to them, they are generally permitted to return to it.

"Finally, farewell! May God be with you, with your congregation, and with all those kind friends who have so nobly come forward to our assistance.

"John Frederic Oberlin"

I shall also insert the following letter, addressed by Oberlin to a friend in England, about six months after the last. It alludes to the exertions of his predecessor, M. Stouber, and relates some anecdotes, to which reference was made at the commencement of this work, respecting the avidity with which the Scriptures were seized upon at their first introduction into the Ban de la Roche:—an avidity which greatly increased in Oberlin's time, more especially when it became known that he possessed, through the medium of the British and Foreign Bible Society, an ample supply of copies for distribution.

"*Waldbach, June* 17, 1805.

"What shall I say, dearest friend—how shall I thank the honorable Bible Society for the gift of £20 for the spread of the kingdom of Jesus Christ? I will entreat God for a rich blessing upon the Institution, and for wisdom to enable me to dispose of its gift in the most effectual manner.

"You ask if there is a desire for Bibles in

the interior of France. I have various reasons for believing that there is; though my personal observation and knowledge extend to our own neighborhood only.* I must, however, refer to what happened a few years ago. The little Steinthal was formerly the only Protestant spot throughout the whole kingdom of France which enjoyed perfect freedom of religious worship. This the Roman Catholic clergy could hardly bear, nor comprehend how God could permit it; and envy and displeasure were but too visible in the countenances of some of them when they happened to converse with any of our Protestant clergy on the subject. About fifty years ago, God sent my excellent predecessor, the Rev. Mr. Stouber, here; a truly apostolic man, who obtained considerable reputation throughout all the Catholic neighborhood. Many Roman Catholics openly declared of him—'This is a man of God,' and the Lord so blessed his labors that the Steinthal villages began to be distinguished from all the Roman Catholic villages in the vicinity. He sent for fifty French Protestant Bibles from Basle, and lent them in the schools, even with permission to the scholars to take them home. It must be observed that he had them divided into three parts, bound in strong parchment, making one hundred and fifty volumes.

"He also distributed many other good French books. The result of this measure, was that the neighbors were made attentive to the Bible.

* Oberlin *never* went far from home. He had never seen Paris, nor made any journey except to Fribourg and to St. Dizier.

A Roman Catholic one day entered a house in this place, and after some desultory talk, during which time he had carefully cast his eye round the apartment, he espied in the window a thick book with a lock; having heard that Bibles had this appearance, he took it up, looked at the title, and asked, 'Whether one could have such a Bible for a crown?' On receiving an answer in the affirmative, he threw down a crown upon the table, and ran hastily out of the cottage and away to his own village, with the Bible under his arm, to the astonishment of every one. From that time the demand continually increased; several hundred small Bibles from Basle and Biela were partly sold, partly given, and partly lent; and all the Biela Bibles in folio, as well as many in quarto, were procured from Switzerland, and dispersed among the Roman Catholics. Yet many copies were taken by the Romish priests from their people and *burnt;* sometimes a violent contention took place about it.

"A priest once surprised one of his people over the Bible, snatched it from him with bitter reproaches, and was going off with it; when the man, who possessed some spirit, and had often heard from his neighbors of the priest's taking away their Bibles, jumped up, snatched his hanger, placed himself before the door and cried out: 'Reverend Sir, replace the Bible on the table. I respect your character; but a thief is no pastor. I will certainly cut you in pieces, rather than suffer you to steal a Bible which has been kindly lent me.' The priest restored the Bible, but ordered the man to return it to the owner; and thus many were returned to us.

"Before the Revolution, I never gave any Bibles to the Roman Catholics with my own hands, but always through those of my parishioners; since the Revolution I have had more freedom, so that I may even let the Roman Catholics take the sacrament in our church, a circumstance that has often happened.* Now, the priests excite a suspicion about the Swiss Bibles, so that many of their people do not know what to do respecting them. I am, however, in hopes of soon procuring some of the Protestant Bibles, which are now printing at Paris. About a fortnight ago, I had the unexpected pleasure of receiving the thanks of an emigrant ex-priest for a Parisian New Testament. I wrote him that I should readily offer him a whole Bible, had I any other than a Swiss edition, which might appear to him suspicious, though it was so to none who examined it by the original. He replied he would thankfully accept it. At last he came to me in person, and also took a German Bible, and some other German books, having learnt German during his emigration. I beg leave to add that many French gentlemen of respectability have ac-

"Oberlin's tolerance," says the Rev. F. Cunningham "was almost unbounded. He administered the Sacrament to Catholics, Lutherans and Calvinists at the sam time, and, because they would not eat the same bread, he had, on the plate, bread of different kinds, wafer, leavened and unleavened. In every thing the same spirit appeared; and it extended not only to his Catholic, but also to his Jewish neighbors, and made him many friends among them all."

cepted Bibles from me with, apparently, sincere joy; and lately a lady came several leagues on horseback in order to request one of me."

Athough through Oberlin's agency the Holy Scriptures were not only circulated abroad, but also among all the Protestants in his extensive parishes, and in the surrounding Roman Catholic villages, there was not at this time any *regularly constituted* Bible Society in the Ban de la Roche.

"The inhabitants of the differeut villages," says Mr. Rauscher,* "seem to be actuated by some secret and spontaneous movement. They assemble together in the evening of certain days, when, after reading a few chapters of the Bible, they all kneel down and join in imploring the divine blessing upon the whole village, as well as upon the parish at large, and upon every institution designed to circulate the truths of the gospel and to bring people nearer to God. They then make a collection, which is deposited in a box kept for the purpose, and reserved there till the time arrives for transmitting it to those Bible and Missionary Societies whose annual reports show that they stand in the greatest need."

A reference to those reports will prove that the collections made on some of these occaions, amounted to very considerable sums.†

* Frederica Bienvenue, Oberlin's youngest daughter who was married, in the year 1806, to the Rev. Mr Rauscher, of Barr.

† See the 3d, 5th, 6th, and 7th Annual Reports of the Protestant Paris Bible Society, &c.

Having been themselves refreshed, and cheered, and comforted, by the perusal of the Sacred Volume, Oberlin's parishioners contributed their little *donations* in aid of the great cause, with a liberality and readiness that proved they were influenced in doing so, by that spirit of love which the blessed gospel inculcates.—Their own moral wilderness had been made to " rejoice and blossom as the rose," by the vivifying rays of the Sun of Righteousness, and they naturally and earnestly desired that *other* " waste places might break forth into joy and sing together," and that the " Word of the Lord might have free course and be glorified."

I will conclude this chapter with the following sweet little letter, addressed by Pastor Oberlin to his scholars, on their having presented him with some garlands in remembrance of the 70th anniversary of his birth.

" *Waldbach, September* 16*th*, 1810.

" My dear Scholars,

"I am very sensible of the honor you have intended me, in sending your garlands as a token of your remembrance of my 70th birthday, completed the 31st of last August. You seem, however, to have forgotten that an honor which one is conscious of not deserving, is in itself humiliating and abasing. If, by my feeble exertions, I have been enabled to be of some utility to you, all the honor belongs to God, who has kindled in my heart the love I bear you, and who has given and preserved my strength till this period to carry forward my heart's desire, which is your good.

"The beautiful flowers with which your great Creator adorned our country, gave you the means of presenting me with this testimony of your united love. These flowers will very soon fade, but the impression they have made on my heart will never die, and I earnestly pray that you may become unfading flowers in the Paradise of God.

"May he bless you, and may he bless the persons who labor for your instruction, with perseverance and faithfulness, that you may prosper, and become useful in the service of our dear and beloved Savior.

"But I have still one wish:—a wish that though I am *old* in years is always *fresh* in my heart:—a wish that reigns predominant in my thoughts and never forsakes me. It is that my parish might make one solemn feast before God, a general and universal dedication, and one in which all persons without distinction might partake, every one according to his respective ability. That is, a dedication of the *heart*, in honor and remembrance of, and in faith in Him, who shed his blood for us in Gethsemane, and permitted himself to be smitten, scourged, and spit upon, crowned with thorns, and nailed to the cross, that we might receive the heaven which our sins had forfeited.—This is the dedication that I so much desire every soul in my parish might join together to make,—even the surrender of himself to Jesus, each one as he is, with all his faults, with all his sins, in order to find in Him, pardon, righteousness, sanctification and redemption.

"Your affectionate Papa,
"JOHN FREDERIC OBERLIN."

CHAPTER VII.

Henry Oberlin's removal to Riga—His sister Henrietta's marriage—Their return to Waldbach—Letter from Oberlin to P. J. Heisch, Esq.—Letter from Henry Oberlin to ditto—Mr. Legrand's settlement in the Ban de la Roche—Introduction of cotton-spinning; silk ribbon manufactory, &c.—Termination of a long impending law-suit—Henry Oberlin's death—His father's resignation on that occasion, displayed in a letter to Mr. Heisch.

In the year 1808, Henry Gottfried Oberlin, who has been already mentioned as his father's active coadjutor in the distribution of Bibles, left the Protestant theological school at Strasbourg, of which he had for the last two years been superintendent, and went to reside as private tutor in the family of Count Richter, at Riga.

His sister Henrietta likewise removed into Russia during the same year, having married the Rev. Mr. Graff, a missionary on the banks of the Wolga.

Oberlin's advancing age, and increasing inability for that very active exertion which the peculiar situation of his parish required, and which he had been accustomed to use, induced the former, however, in the year 1813, and Mr. and Mrs. Graff, with their family of young children, in the subsequent one, to come and take up their residence again under the paternal roof at Waldbach.

The following note, addressed by Oberlin to P. J. Heisch, Esq., speaks of his own increasing weakness, and alludes, with grateful pleasure, to Henry's return.

"Dear, not to be forgotten friend!

"On the 5th of December, God restored to me my son Henry Gottfried from Russia, who now relieves me from part of my labor, though there is still so much left to be done that *six* of us could find ample employment. Your remembrance and letter have given me exceeding joy, and I only regret the impossibility of having answered you before. My situation is unique in its way; and my labor seems to increase as my strength decreases, especially the strength of my eyes. For these several years past I have been repeatedly threatened with sudden death.* Now, thank God, I am very well.

* Oberlin had a most extraordinary and serious illness during the period of the Revolution, in 1794, supposed to be brought on by over-exertion, and he never appeared to have entirely overcome the shock that his constitution underwent. The prevailing disposition of the mind sometimes displays itself during the intervals of delirium and, whilst his fever lasted, he often distressed poor Louisa, by perpetually calling upon her to bring him thousands and thousands for the furtherance of his plans. He used often to speak afterwards of the state of his mind during this illness, and of the distinct ideas he had been enabled to form of the difference between the natural and spiritual man.

"May God be with you, dear and not to be forgotten friend, and with your dear family. It gives me no concern to think that we shall not see each other again in this world;—in the next our intercourse will be more frequent, more easy, and more delightful. Adieu.

"Your aged friend of seventy-three,

"J. F. OBERLIN.

"My sincere respects to the Rev. Dr. Steinkopff."

Henry also wrote to Mr. Heisch about the same time, and as his letter contains some particulars of his truly interesting family, and of various circumstances to which I shall afterwards have to refer, I insert it.

"*Waldbach, December 11th*, 1813.

"Highly honored Sir, my valued friend, and former teacher,

"My father received your friendly letter on the 10th of April, and he allows me the pleasure of replying to part of it.

"The Steinthal has, during the last few years, witnessed many melancholy, but also many cheering events. Conflagrations, formerly so rare, have destroyed many houses in most of the villages; even the beautiful parsonage of Rothau fell, a few years ago, a prey to the flames. We have also lost since that perio several of the most worthy inhabitants of ou valley, who, both in word and deed, were brigh and shining examples to their contemporaries; —such were, for instance, Catharine Gagnière, and Catharine Banzet. We must likewise include among our apparent adversities the cir cumstance of cotton-spinning having been on the decline for several years, and as a similar circumstance occurs with regard to weaving, many families have been thrown into great distress. But God, who has always had an open eye upon the Steinthal, and extended a helping hand towards it, has also manifested himself in the present juncture. Besides the excellent magistrates (*maires*) with whom the whole of my dear father's parish is blessed, God has given us, in the person of the Count Lezay Marnesia, a prefect who entertains an extraordinary affection for the people of the Steinthal. Through his means in particular, and the striking interposition of Providence, the long pending law-suit about the forests, which had been so oppressive to the inhabitants, has been brought to an amicable conclusion this year. It also pleased God to send, a short time since, a gentleman into this country who formerly kept a *ribbon* manufactory in Alsace, and who takes a great interest in effectually assisting the inhabitants of the Steinthal. Our good and excellent Louisa Schepler is still alive, and always, in conjunction with my dear father, observing the same fidelity and self-devotion in the performance of her duties. We, his children, have been very much dispersed, but we were much more so a little time ago than we are now. It is, indeed, remarkable how we are concentrated in the Steinthal. My brother Charles has been for some years past clergyman of Rothau.* My sister Frederica, who married

* Charles Conserve, Oberlin's second son, was born in 1776. In the year 1803, he married Sophia Catharine

the Rev. Mr. Rauscher, now resides at Barr where Mr. Rauscher keeps a school, and also exercises his ministerial functions. I am myself, in fine, come to the Steinthal from Russia, or Livonia, though not by the shortest way. I wrote to you, respected friend, from Riga, under the date of August 2nd, 1811. I wrot also, at a later period, to Dr. Steinkopff, but never received an answer from your country. I ought to have mentioned above, that the gentleman who is introducing the ribbon manufactory into the Steinthal is a native of Basle; perhaps he is not unknown to you. It is Mr. Legrand, who was formerly a member of the Directory in Switzerland. My dear sister Louisa Charité is married to a good worthy man, the Rev. Peter Witz, of Colmar. She, as well as dear Frederica, has several children, and so also has sister Henrietta, in Russia. Our beloved sister Fidelité has been for several years lost to us in this world, which grieves *me*, in particular, even now.—The good Fidelité—what a faithful sister she was!—as faithful a sister as she was a mother and wife.*

Franck, of Strasbourg, the widow of an officer named Berard. On account of his father's advancing age, he was induced, in 1806, to relieve him of part of his pastoral duties, by accepting the living of Rothau, at which place he still resides.

* Fidelité Caroline Oberlin was married, in 1795, to the Rev. James Wolff, of Mittelbergheim. She died May 9th, 1809, leaving two little girls, who soon followed their mother to the grave. Her death was a great affliction to her near connexions, but especially to Henry, to whom she was remarkably endeared, and to her father. In speaking of this circumstance, Mr. Heisch, the long

"I shall now conclude, as it is possible that my dear father and Louisa may wish to add a word themselves.

"I remain ever, your grateful old pupil and friend,

"HENRY GOTTFRIED OBERLIN."

Although on Oberlin's first arrival in the Ban de la Roche, the population consisted of eighty or a hundred families only, it increased in the course of a few years to five or six hundred, constituting altogether three thousand souls.

To provide employment for so great a number of persons, even supposing that five hundred could be employed during four or five months of the year in the cultivation of land, and that one third were infants and infirm persons incapable of work, became a most important object, and gave rise to the introduction of various branches of mechanical industry, adapted to local circumstances; such, for instance, as *straw-platting*, *knitting*, and *dying* with the

---

and intimate friend of the family, says, "I particularly recollect the warm attachment that subsisted between Oberlin's daughter Fidelitè, his son Henry, and himself. Oh, he did love his children most tenderly! If I am not mistaken, I saw him weep but once, and that was when he married his daughter Fidelité to Mr. Wolff. Tears of joy in the prospect of her happiness, were then mingled with those tears of grief, which a separation from this beloved child could not but occasion. Some time after he repeatedly visited her at Mittelbergheim, and I had once or twice the pleasure of accompanying him. It is scarcely possible for any one, who was not an eye-witness to this scene, to form an idea of the tender affection that subsisted between father and daughter."

plants of the country. The former was introduced by an invalid captain, whose gratitude for the kind reception he met with, on soliciting the hospitality of the generous pastor of Waldbach, induced him to proffer his services in furthering the views of his benefactor, by instructing the young persons in an art with which necessity had previously made him acquainted.

Besides these employments, Oberlin had succeeded in introducing the spinning of cotton by the hand; and, as he gave prizes to the best spinners in addition to their wages, this branch of industry for a time succeeded so well that it once gained for the Ban de la Roche, in the course of a single year, and from one manufacturer, the emolument of 32,000 francs—an enormous sum, considering the extreme poverty and indigence to which the inhabitants had but just before been subjected. Weaving followed, and, notwithstanding numerous obstacles, promised a large increase of pecuniary means; but, unfortunately, the introduction of machinery at Schirmeck and some of the surrounding villages, produced an entire revolution about the time the preceding letter was written, deprived them of this source of maintenance, and seemed likely to reduce them to their former state of necessity and want.

During this emergency, Mr. Legrand, of Basle, formerly one of the Directors of the Helvetic Republic, and of whom Henry makes grateful mention, attracted to the Ban de la Roche by regard and affection for its pastor, and the simplicity, intelligence and integrity of his parishioners, persuaded his two sons, to whom he had relinquished business, to remove their manufactory of silk ribbons from the department of the Upper Rhine to Foudai, believing that its introduction in the Steinthal, by giving employ to a great number of hands, would become not only an advantage but a real blessing to the peasantry there, who were at this period sadly in need of work. The first invasion of the allies, who took possession of their workshops, induced Mr. Daniel and Mr. Joseph Legrand to accede, without hesitation, to the wishes of their father, and indeed proved a means of hastening their removal.*

In the course of a short time, through the exertions of this benevolent and highly respectable family, industry and happiness again smiled in the valley:—for whilst the introduction of the silk manufactory caused trade to be carried on with renewed vigor, and gave employment to several hundred hands, it was attended with another great advantage, too seldom experienced in manufacturing districts; this was that the ribbon looms were distributed about the houses in the different villages, so that, contrary to the usual custom, the children could remain whilst at work under the eye of

* The name of Daniel Legrand is well known in connexion with the Paris Bible Society, to which he has ong been a warm and zealous friend. Having himself experienced, in a striking manner, the renovating influence of religion, he now takes every opportunity of inducing others, as far as lies in his power, to become "followers of Jesus," and to embrace those truths which form the ground of his own faith and practice.

their parents, instead of being exposed to the contaminating influence of bad example.

"Conducted by Providence," says Mr. Legrand, in a letter addressed to the Baron de Gérando, "into this remote valley, I was the more struck with the sterility of its soil, its straw-thatched cottages, the apparent poverty of its inhabitants, and the simplicity of their fare (chiefly consisting of potatoes) from the contrast which these external appearances formed to the cultivated conversation which I enjoyed with almost every individual I met whilst traversing its five villages, and the frankness and *naivete* of the children, who extended to me their little hands. I had often heard of Pastor Oberlin, and eagerly sought his acquaintance. He gave me the most hospitable reception, and anticipated my desire to know more of the history of the little colony whose manners had surprised me so greatly, by placing in my hands the annals of his parish.* I there found an unconnected, but detailed history of the institutions for general instruction founded by his predecessor, and continued by himself.

"It is now four years since I removed here with my family; and the pleasure of residing in the midst of a people, whose manners are softened and whose minds are enlightened by the instructions which they receive from their earliest infancy, more than reconciles us to the privations which we must necessarily experi-

* The Annals of the Ban de la Roche were commenced by Oberlin in 1770.

ence in a valley separated from the rest of the world by a chain of surrounding mountains."*

With regard to the long impending law-suit mentioned in the preceding letter from Henry Oberlin to Mr. Heisch, it seems necessary to give some explanation, more especially as it will afford another proof, in addition to the many already adduced, that the almost unbounded influence which Oberlin had acquired over his people, was always exerted for purposes of beneficence. The litigation, to which that letter refers, had been carried on for upwards of eighty years, between the peasantry of the Ban and the *seigneurs* of the territory, with respect to the right of the forests which covered the greater part of the mountains. This ruinous contest, which impoverished both parties by an enormous expense, and discouraged improvement, had survived even the French Revolution, which swept away in a moment so many absurd remnants of ancient feudalism. M. de Lezay Marnesia,† prefect of the Lower Rhine, who deeply lamented the disgraceful contention,

* M. Legrand soon became a most useful auxiliary to Oberlin, devoting his leisure hours to benevolent purposes. The superintendence and direction of the schools, which he managed in a very superior manner, particularly claimed his attention; and so great was his ardor in the work, that he was once about to take up his residence for the seven winter months in Belmont school, had not his health prevented it.

† M. de Lezay Marnesia entertained a peculiar affection and respect for Oberlin, although differing from him in his religious tenets. He would sometimes consult him on the sceptical objections to revealed religion which presented themselves to his mind, and appeared as well pleased to yield as Oberlin was to gain the victory in argument.

and earnestly desired to see it terminated, at length opened his mind to Oberlin on the subject, and entreated him to use every effort in his power for the restoration of peace, declaring that he knew no other person so capable of effecting it. The latter readily acceded to his wishes, for it was what he himself had long and ardently desired, though the impossibility of accomplishing it, until sanctioned by the authority of the magistrate, had hitherto prevented his taking an active part in the business.* No sooner had he received this intimation, than he began to take every opportunity of convincing his parishioners, in private conversation, that this litigation was the scourge of the country; assuring them that a voluntary sacrifice on their part, for the sake of peace, would be far preferable to the uncertainties of a prolonged law-suit, and that the end they wished to gain could only be obtained by a succession of the most wearisome debates. Nor was it in private conversation only that he urged his plea, for in the pulpit also he frequently insisted on the duty of avoiding subjects of dispute, and on the characteristics of that charity "which suffereth long and is kind, seeketh not her own, beareth all things."

Having, in this manner, prepared his parishioners to listen to his proposal, and when he saw that they were ready to receive it, he frankly declared his conviction that they were bound as much by their interest as their duty to consent to an accommodation.

---

* Oberlin had had for several years this motto affixed to one of his doors. "O Gott erbarme Dich des Steinthals, und mache dem Prozess ein Ende." ("O God, have mercy on the Steinthal, and put an end to the law-suit!")

His advice was followed. The parties acceded to an agreement advantageous to both sides. What so many years had not been able to effect, Oberlin—the mild and gentle Oberlin—brought about by a few conciliatory words. The prefect was desirous that the inhabitants should not be allowed to forget to whom they were indebted for the restoration of peace. At his suggestion, the mayors in deputation presented to their pastor the pen with which M. de Lezay had signed the solemn engagement, entreating him to suspend it in his study as a trophy of the victory which habitual beneficence, and the exercise of the Christian graces, had enabled him to gain over long continued animosity and bad feeling. He modestly complied with their request, and was often heard to say that the day on which the pen was used, June 6th, 1813, was one of the happiest of his life.*

I must now advert to an affecting event, which happened in Oberlin's family in the winter of 1817. This was the death of his son Henry Gottfried, who had only resided under the paternal roof for about three years after his return from Russia, before he was summoned hence, to taste, as we have every reason to believe, of the joys of heaven.

"God's ways are not our ways, neither are his thoughts our thoughts;" and it sometimes pleases him to remove to a better country, and to a higher state of existence, those whom we had fondly imagined would become as shining lights in the world, and instruments devoted to his ser-

* For several years this memorable pen retained its station in his study; but it at length disappeared, without any one being able to tell what had become of it.

vice; as though to remind us that he can effect his own purposes in what way, and in what manner he sees best, without the aid of short-sighted, and, at the best, fallible creatures like ourselves.

The immediate occasion of Henry's death was supposed to arise from a cold, which he took in assisting to extinguish a fire that had broken out in the night in a town on his route, as he was making, in 1816, a circuit of eighteen hundred miles in the south of France, with a view to inspect the state of the Protestant churches, and to ascertain the means of supplying them more generally with the Holy Scriptures.

The fatigue attending the remainder of the journey, added to the seeds of incipient disease, had so shattered his constitution, that, soon after arriving in his native valley, he was induced to remove to Rothau, instead of remaining at Waldbach, in order to receive the benefit of his brother Charles's advice, who, in addition to his clerical functions, was a medical practitioner. On perceiving, however, that the complaint rapidly gained ground, he desired, with the greatest resignation and composure, to be conveyed home again to his father's house, that he might die there.

So universally was Oberlin beloved, that his parishioners seized every opportunity of proving their attachment to him and to his family; and on this occasion a truly affecting scene presented itself. No sooner was Henry's request made known in the village, than twelve peasants immediately presented themselves at the parsonage-house, and offered to carry him upon a litter to Waldbach, which is about six miles distant from Rothau. He could not, however, bear exposure to the open air, and it was therefore found expedient to place him in a covered cart; but, as it slowly proceeded through the valley, the faithful peasants walked before it, carefully removing every stone, that the beloved invalid might experience as little inconvenience as possible from jolting over the rough roads.

A few weeks after his arrival under the paternal roof, his life, which had promised such extensive usefulness, drew near its close. Faith, mingled with pious resignation to the will of his heavenly Father, who was thus early pleased to call him to himself, was strikingly exhibited in his last moments, and on the 16th of November, 1817, without a struggle or a sigh, he "sweetly slept in Jesus."*

A few particulars of his close are given in the notes of the sermon which his father preached on the occasion of his death. I shall here insert a translation of them, from the original MSS.

"My son Henry Gottfried, in the midst of distressing bodily anguish, (for as to his mental powers, he enjoyed the full and clear use of them till the last moment of his life,) and under the pressure of acute and lingering sufferings, often said, 'Oh mercy! mercy! Oh God! hast thou then ceased to be merciful?—Oh, it is a hard, hard, hard thing to die!'

---

* His premature and lamented death is thus recorded in the Fourteenth Report of the British and Foreign Bible Society: "Your committee think it due to the late Rev. Henry Oberlin, of Waldbach, in Alsace, to bear their testimony to that zeal by which he was urged to sacrifice his valuable life in exertions for distributing the Holy Scriptures among his countrymen."

"Half or quarter of an hour before expiring, his countenance exhibited less suffering, and he said, (although with considerable difficulty,) 'Now a little repose—a little consolation—a little joy.' Then he often repeated, 'From death unto life'—'From death unto life.'

"At length he presented his trembling hand to place it in mine; he pressed mine very sensibly and retained it in his own, 'from death unto life,' for without our perceiving it he ceased to breathe. Twice, believing him gone, Louisa Schepler closed his eyes, but they opened again, and were raised on high."

Henry Oberlin was buried in the church-yard of Foudai, where a monument of wood, surrounded by willows, is erected to his memory.

His venerable father was graciously supported under this heavy stroke, and in his discourse over the grave of his son, spoke tenderly and familiarly of the departed, as having only preceded them a little way in their pilgrimage, soon to be overtaken, and for ever reunited to those whom he had left behind. The following letter to his friend Mr. Heisch, exhibits the disinterested manner in which he contemplated his own irreparable loss, when dwelling upon his son's removal to eternal glory.

"*Waldbach, in the Steinthal, Jan.* 8, 1818

"Accept, my dear, not to be forgotten friend my sincere and heartfelt thanks for the many proofs of your continued affectionate remembrance. Your name is inscribed on my heart; and yet I find it difficult to give you any assurance of it, being extremely engaged with labors that are continually increasing, whilst the use of my bodily powers is greatly diminished. I particularly suffer in my eyes, which sometimes altogether refuse me their service, notwithstanding the excellent spectacles you presented to me, and one pair of which Louisa gratefully uses.

"We all sincerely rejoiced at the departure of our Henry from this world; for besides having been subjected during his whole life to a chain of complicated sufferings, he had suffered for some months past (ever since his missionary journey in France) with peculiar severity, so that his emaciated appearance awakened every one's sympathy, and neither medicines nor any thing else could procure him any real alleviation or respite from pain. In consequence of the warm recommendations of our friends, we were induced to call in Dr. Stückalberger, a very clever physician of Basle, a few weeks before our Henry's decease; but no sooner had he seen him, and become acquainted with his symptoms, than he said, 'I shall not touch dear Mr. Oberlin with any medicine or remedy, nay, not even with medical advice, being perfectly convinced that if, on the one hand, I may hope to effect any good, or even may effect it, I shall, on the other hand, do more harm than it may again be in my power to remedy." This was both kind and judicious; and I had been endeavoring to persuade the other hysicians to adopt the same plan, though in vain; for, with the utmost kindness, they were resolved to do all in their power to assist him. God had, in this case, reserved to himself the exclusive prerogative of affording effectual help. Henry, in addition to that spirit of universal benevolence by which he was animated, felt a peculiar interest for two nations, Livonia, together with the whole of Russia, and France. No doubt our and his good Lord now assigns to him some more extensive sphere of activity than he could have had here, not only, perhaps, for the benefit of these two nations, but even for that of other nations and other individuals. May we be his servants; no matter whether here or there, if w can but be faithful in his service, and of some utility to others!

"Henry received your letter of the 17th of October, as well as the elegant silver pencil-cases, and commissioned me to return you his sincerest thanks. He gave them as a remembrance of you to his brother Charles Conservé, clergyman of Rothau, who has shown him extraordinary kindness both as a physician and a brother.

"Louisa Schepler and all our dear friends here, thank you cordially for your remembrance, and assure you of their uninterrupted affection and recollection.

"God grant that you may become useful in his service.

"Adieu, my long endeared friend!

"JOHN FREDERIC OBERLIN."

CHAPTER VIII.

Medal presented to Oberlin by the Royal Agricultural Society of Paris—Oberlin's private character—His description of himself—Mr. Owen's letter, containing an account of a Ban de la Roche Sabbath—Oberlin's ministry—Sermons—Ministerial labors, &c.—His paternal influence over his flock—Questions addressed to his parishioners—Circulars.

NOTWITHSTANDING Oberlin's advancing age, and the loss he had experienced in the death of his son, the Ban de la Roche still witnessed a succession of useful improvements, and a progress in civilization and prosperity. So much delighted were his friends at Strasbourg and at Paris with witnessing the success of his indefatigable exertions, that, in the year 1818, they agreed to collect, without his knowledge, documents of the good which he had achieved, and to submit them to the Royal and Central Agricultural Society of Paris.

M. le Comte Francois de Neufchâteau, who had repeatedly visited the Steinthal, was deputed to this office, and requested to propose the vote of a gold medal to the pastor of Waldbach, in acknowledgment of the services which he had rendered, during more than half a century, to agriculture in particular, and to mankind in general.

"If you would behold an instance of what may be effected in any country for the advancement of agriculture and the interests of humanity," said he, when addressing the Society upon this occasion, "quit for a moment the banks of the Seine, and ascend one of the steepest summits of the Vosges mountains. Friends of the plow, and of human happiness, come and behold the Ban de la Roche! Climb with me the rocks so sublimely piled upon each other, which separate this canton from the rest of the world, and though the country and the climate may at first sight appear forbidding, I will venture to promise you an ample recompense for the fatigue of your excursion.

"As for myself, after having formed the administration of the department of the Vosges, in 1790, and presided over it, in 1791, I had, in 1793, to travel over those mountains as a commissioner of the government, at the very period when the parishes of Rothau and Waldbach, before that time dependent on the principality of Salm, were united to the department. I have, therefore, been long acquainted with the valuable services rendered, for more than fifty years, to the Ban de la Roche, by John Frederic Oberlin. Ever since that time, and to the advanced age of seventy-eight, he has persevered in carrying forward the interesting reformation first suggested and commenced by his virtue, piety and zeal. He has refused invitations to more important and more lucrative situations, lest the Ban de la Roche should relapse into its former desolate state; and by his extraordinary efforts and unabated exertions, he averted from his parishioners, in the years 1812, 1816, and 1817, the horrors of approaching famine.*

* The new crop of potatoes that Oberlin had introduced, formed the principal subsistence of the people during those disastrous years, when the season was so cold and rainy that they could not get in two-thirds of the

"Such a benefactor of mankind deserves the veneration and the gratitude of all good men; and it gives me peculiar pleasure to present you with the opportunity of acknowledging, in the person of M. Oberlin, not a single act, but a whole life, devoted to agricultural improvements, and to the diffusion of useful knowledge amongst the inhabitants of a wild and uncultivated district.

* * * * *

* * * * *

"We have already ascertained that there is in France uncultivated land sufficient for the formation of five thousand villages. When we wish to organize these colonies, Waldbach will present a perfect model; and, in the thirty or forty rural hamlets which already exist, there is not one, even amongst the most flourishing, in which social economy is carried to a higher degree of perfection, or in which the annals of the Ban de la Roche may not be studied with advantage."

On the conclusion of this report, the proposed tribute of affectionate gratitude, was, by unanimous consent, awarded to M. Oberlin; upon which the Baron de Gérando, Counsellor of State, to whose care it was consigned, expressed the gratification he should have in presenting it to the

corn at all; and the scarcity so great, that poor little children, exhausted with hunger, were seen to drop down n the streets. A sack of wheat during that time of distress rose to 145 francs, and the potatoes to nearly one sou apiece.

The precise acquaintance which the inhabitants of the Ban de la Roche had acquired, through Oberlin's assistance, with the vegetable productions of their canton, was believed to be the means of preventing the most distressing diseases.

venerable pastor, not only because he regarded it as an act of justice due to his extraordinary services, but also because it would afford such great pleasure to the inhabitants of the Vosges valleys, to find their beloved benefactor, guide, counsellor and friend, regarded as an individual deserving of this token of public admiration and gratitude.

But whilst Oberlin was thus gaining the meed of universal applause by his acts of public beneficence, his domestic virtues were endearing him more and more to his family circle, where they always displayed themselves in the most truly amiable light. I shall, therefore, now reverse the picture, and present my readers with a view of Oberlin in his personal and more private, as well as in his ministerial character. In this he will be found to shine as brightly as in his public capacity; thereby manifesting the pureness and the extent of that Christian principle, which constrained not only the great movements of his life, but his minutest actions.

Oberlin, in his person, was handsome, rather under the usual height, but remarkably dignified in his appearance. There was, however, nothing affected in his manner of carrying himself. His outward garb was evidently the mark of the master mind within him. Dressed, as he usually was when out of doors, in a cocked hat, and with a red ribbon at his chest, the decoration of the Legion of Honor,* his air was so imposing

* This decoration was awarded to Oberlin by Louis XVIII. in acknowledgment of the services he had rendered to an extensive population. "The king," he used to say, "has had the goodness to send me this decoration; but what have I done to merit it? Who, in my situation.

as to call forth the attention and respect of every one who saw him. His manner was grave, but affectionate; condescending, but in the highest degree gentlemanly. His courtesy towards his parishioners was constantly testified. He did not pass those amongst them who were grown up, without pulling off his hat and speaking a few words of kindness: nor any of the children without shaking them by the hand, or showing them some little act of attention. "Jesus," he often said, "loved children. It is to such as resemble them that he promises the kingdom of heaven." He was always extremely anxious, in every part of his conduct, to prevent the possibility of misconstruction on the part of those over whom he watched. "On one occasion," says one of my friends who visited the Ban de la Roche a few years ago, "as we were walking up a hill, he had the arm of his son-in-law, whilst my wife was walking alone. Fearing this might be considered self-indulgent or disrespectful by some of his younger parishioners, whom he happened to pass, he stopped to make an apology to them for this apparent disregard of the law of civility and kindness."*

His manner of accosting his inferiors was perfectly unique. "When our postilion, who appeared to have some previous acquaintance with the Ban de la Roche, met him," continues the same friend, "he and the old man were instantly

---

would not have acted as I have done, and perhaps better still?"

* It must be remembered that Oberlin was then in his eightieth year.

with their hats lowered to the ground, whilst Ober-lin stepped forward to shake him by the hand, and to make some inquiry about his friends at Strasbourg. This was done with all the sweetness of Christian feeling, whilst there was no departure from the dignity with which his situation and circumstances naturally invested him. Goo manners prevailed in these valleys to an exten that is rarely witnessed. The practice of the pastor produced the happiest effects upon the mass of population. The habitual politeness of the French character might have assisted in this work, but I have never witnessed in any other poor people such remarkable and universal suavity:—such complete refinement as in these hardy mountaineers.

"As the Dear Father had the highest regard for his people, so he had the best opinion of their skill, and wondered that any one should doubt about it. I happened one day, when we were driven by a man who seemed to go on in a hazardous manner, to say 'Prenez garde,' (take care.) The old man appeared hurt at this admonition, both on my account and on that of the driver. He assured me that all was safe, and at the end of our drive, took the greatest pains to prevent any feeling of vexation which might arise in the mind of his parishioner."

Oberlin's habits were very *orderly*. Every thing seemed to have its place in his house. There was a box to deposit every morsel of litter, and which could only be of service in the stove. His books, a great number of which were in manuscript, were perfectly arranged, and written in a beautiful hand, for it was a point of duty with him, as before stated by Mr. Legrand, to give every letter its perfect formation. His Bible was marked throughout with different colored ink, according to the application which he, in the course of his reading, had made of different passages.

In conversation he was fluent and very unreserved; willing to communicate all he knew, and, on the other hand, inquisitive as to every thing which he saw, and from which it appeared likely he could derive information.

His *activity* was as astonishing as his zeal; he never rode on horseback if he could help it, still less in the inside of a carriage; and was accustomed, till prevented by increasing infirmity, to climb the steepest summits of the Vosges, or penetrate through pathless snows, regardless of cold or danger, in order to visit the sick, and administer religious consolation to the dying; often too, after all the varied and arduous duties of the day, would he travel to Strasbourg in the night to procure medicines, or to obtain assistance or information from his friends in that city, that not a day might be lost to the interests of his beloved Steinthal.*

The superiority of his intellectual powers appeared in all he said and in all he did; and he

* Oberlin was, at one time, not only minister, schoolmaster, farmer, and mechanic; but also general physician to his parish; the knowledge which he had acquired of medicine during his residence in Mr. Ziegenhagen's family having qualified him for the post. He also learned to open *veins*, and established a *dispensary;* and when his ministerial functions would no longer allow of his devoting so much time to the purpose as it required, he delegated the office to his son Charles, and to a young man of talent whom he had sent to study at Strasbourg.

possessed great influence over others, every body loving and obeying him absolutely, though without servility. His mind was of a modest kind, yet of a very energetic and decided order; though, as he seldom, if ever, went from home, he had seen little of the world, and, except in his younge years, read little but his Bible. His conversatio was never more eloquent, nor his views more ex panded, than when he talked on the subject of the extension of the kingdom of God, and when he narrated to his boys, as he would frequently do, particulars of the life and adventures of Dr. Vanderkemp, the missionary, Vincent de Paul, and others, by which means he riveted their attention and excited the warmest feelings of their hearts. His views of religion were of a very simple and elevated cast: "no cloud of doubt crossed the serene atmosphere of his tranquil joys:"—he continually looked at God as his "Heavenly Father," present with him, and rested all his hopes in Jesus, "the Author and Finisher of our faith."

His dependence upon his Heavenly Father made him order all the events of his life, in which he felt any difficulty in deciding, by *lot;* for this purpose he kept two little tickets, with yea and nay upon them, in his pocket, and these, with prayer, he was continually in the habit of using.*

Oberlin, as it may perhaps be supposed, was a great physiognomist as well as a phrenologist and the system of Gall had in him a zealous par tisan; he was also a warm admirer and disciple

* Oberlin bequeathed his lot-box, the token of his peculiar faith, to the Rev. Mr. Blumhardt, of the Missionary Institution at Basle.

of his friend Lavater,* and had collected a great number of *silhouettes*, both of friends and strangers, under which he wrote his opinion, always

* In the year 1795, Henry Oberlin paid a visit at Zurich, and became acquainted with Lavater, in whose family he was received with more than ordinary affection. This acquaintance laid the foundation of the tenderest and most intimate friendship between Oberlin and that distinguished individual, which terminated only with the life of the latter. He died at Zurich, where he had resided the greater part of his life, January 2, 1801, in consequence of a wound which he received from a French soldier, whom, at the time of the siege, he ran out to separate from another with whom he was scuffling. After lingering in agony for more than a twelvemonth, during which time he evinced, by his patience and cheerfulness, the power of that principle which in life had made him so active, he resigned his soul into the hands of his Creator.

Lavater was a man of extraordinary powers, and universally beloved by all classes of people. He was as much known in his own country as a zealous and devoted Christian minister, as he is in this country by his study of physiognomy. This latter study, he used to say, was taken up for little more than amusement.

The following note, written during the period of his illness, to Henry Oberlin, who was at that time also suffering from indisposition, is a proof of the sweet and resigned state of his mind:

"*Erlenbach, Feb. 1st*, 1800.

"Dear Oberlin,

"We must both humble ourselves under the chastising and fatherly hand of God. It will be good for us both to be led in this way, and no other. Let us look forward with hope, and expect the best, nor doubt his goodness one moment. We cannot be better led than we are. If we possess health, God of his love bestows it; if sickness he ordains that it should be so. We have nothing to fear His love will never forsake us; but will continue to direct us to one goal—even to himself."

an indulgent one, of the talents and general character of the individual.

There was a striking simplicity and artlessness in his character, which occasionally led him to speak of himself, and of his own actions, in a manner that some might attribute to egotism; but this was far from being the case, for few individuals could be more truly humble, or disclaim all merits of their own more sincerely than he did. He wrote the following description of his own character, to place beneath a profile, which was cut out and highly approved by himself.* It will account for the preceding remarks.

"A strange compound of contradictory qualities. I do not yet exactly know what I am to make of myself. I am intelligent; and yet possessed of very limited powers:—prudent and more politic than my fellow clergymen; but also very apt to blunder, especially when in the least excited. I am firm, yet of a yielding disposition; and both of these, in certain cases, to a great degree. I am not only daring, but actually courageous; whilst, at the same time, I am often in secret very cowardly. I am very upright and sincere, yet also very complaisant to men, and in a degree, therefore, insincere. I am a German and a Frenchman; noble, generous, ready to render service, faithful, very grateful,—deeply affected by the least benefit or kindness, which is ever after engraven on my heart; and yet again flighty and indifferent. I am irritable to a formidable degree. He who treats me generously

* Oberlin presented this profile to the Rev. Francis Cunningham, during his visit at Waldbach, in 1820.

soon gains the ascendency over me; but opposition creates in me an astonishing degree of firmness, especially in matters of conscience. I have a lively imagination, but no memory, properly speaking. The histories which I have taken pains to impress on my mind remain with me, but dates and the names of persons I often forget the next day, notwithstanding all the pains I have taken to remember them. I used to speak Latin fluently and even elegantly, but now I cannot utter three or four words together. I make selections from books, and instruct others in some branch of science for a long time; but a few years after, my scholars, even if they know nothing more than what I taught them, may in their turn become my teachers, and the books from which I made extracts (with the exception of those of a certain description) appear wholly new to me.

"I habitually work my way through my studies till I obtain clear ideas; but if I wish to penetrate deeper, every thing vanishes before me. I have a great talent for removing difficulties in order to render every thing smooth and easy to myself, and to every body else. I am so extremely sensitive, tender, and compassionate, that I can find neither words nor expressions corresponding to my feelings, so that the latter almost overpower me, and occasion me acute pain. I am always busy and industrious, but also fond of ease and indolence. I am generally quick in resolving, and equally so in executing. I have a peculiar esteem for the female sex. I am a very great admirer of painting, music, and poetry, and yet I have no skill in any of them. Mechanics, natural history, and so forth, constitute my favor ite studies. I am very fond of regularity, and of arranging and classifying, but my weak memory, added to constant employment, renders it difficult to me. I am given to planning and scheming, and yet endeavor, in my peculiar way to do things in the best manner.

"I am a genuine soldier, but I was more s before my bodily powers were so much weakened; I was formerly anxious to be the foremost in danger, and the firmest in pain, but have now lost that desire. From my childhood I have felt a longing and preponderating desire for a higher state of existence, and therefore a wish for death. I am the greatest admirer of military order and subordination, not however in a spirit of slavery, but of that noble affectionate attachment which compels the coward to show courage, and the disorderly to be punctual. I feel no obstinacy or disinclination to yield to strong internal conviction, but on the other hand a fervent heart-felt joy in yielding to both great and small, high and low, gentlemen and peasants, children and servants, and thence a willingness to listen and an inclination to suffer myself, if possible, to be convinced. But when I feel no conviction I can never think of yielding. I am humorous and a little witty or satirical, but without intentiona malice."

As the villages of Oberlin's little district wei too far apart to allow of his preaching every week in all of them, he took each of the three churches in rotation, and the peasants made an arrangement to come in turns with a horse every Sunday morning to fetch him, and to take him home to partake of their dinner after the sermon. It was always a festival for every family who could thus entertain the dear father, and afforded him an opportunity of conversing about their temporal and spiritual wants. He made a point, when the little repast was ended, of seeing the *hildren* of the house one by one in succession, according to their age, and of talking to them like an affectionate father, in language adapted to their respective capacities, as well as of making a present to each.

I cannot here refrain from inserting the lively picture which Mr. Owen has drawn, in his own admirable manner, of a Ban de la Roche Sabbath; and in which he also makes an allusion to those three excellent women whose names well deserve to be put upon record with that of their pastor.

"*Basle, Sept.* 16, 1818.

"The place from which my last was dated, Waldbach, has completely filled my mind, and laid such hold on my warmest affections, that I can scarcely bring myself to think, or speak, or write, on any thing but Pastor Oberlin, and his Ban de la Roche. You will remember that the first foreign letter which awakened an interest in our minds—the letter which made its way most directly to our hearts, and which, at the celebration of our First Anniversary, produced the trongest, and, if I may judge of others by myself, the most lasting impression upon us all, was that wherein this venerable pastor reported the distribution he proposed to make of the Bibles assigned to him, and drew, with the hand of a master, the characters of those women who labored with him in the Gospel, and to whom, as the highest remuneration he could bestow, and their ambition coveted, a Bible was to be presented.*

"I cannot describe the sensations with which I entered the mountainous parish, containing five villages and three churches, in which this primitive evangelist, who more than half a century has occupied this station, exercises his functions; and still less those with which I entered his residence, and approached his venerable person. The reception he gave me was such as from the profound humility of his character might have been anticipated. My visit to him and his flock was wholly unexpected; and when I announced to him, in my introduction, that I appeared before him as the Secretary of the British and Foreign Bible Society, to testify, on their part, the respect and affection with which they regarded him, as one of the earliest and most interesting of their foreign correspondents, the good man took me by the hand, and drew me gently towards the seat which he usually occupies, exclaiming, but without any turbulence of either voice or manner,—'Sir, this is too great an honor:—how shall I answer words like these?' After the first emotions had subsided, our conversation became familiar; and as it never ceased, from that time to the moment of our separation, to turn more or less upon the things pertaining to the kingdom of God, as they appeared in the small scale of his own, or the great scale of the Bible Society's labors, it never ceased to be deeply interesting, and pregnant with edification.

---

* See page 132.

"The Sunday exhibited this venerable man in the pastoral character, under which it had been so much my desire, might it but be permitted me, to see him. As he makes the circuit of his churches, the turn on this Sunday belonged to Belmont, distant about half a league from the parsonage of Waldbach. At ten o'clock we began to move. Mr. Oberlin took the lead in his ministerial attire, in a large beaver and flowing wig, mounted on a horse brought for that purpose, according to custom, by one of the bourgeois of the village, whose turn it was to have the honor of fetching his pastor, and receiving him to dinner at his table. I rode as nearly beside him as the narrow track would allow. Mr. Rönneberg, accompanied by Mr. Daniel Legrand, followed. The rear was brought up by the bourgeois before mentioned, carrying a leathern bag, slung across his shoulders, which contained the other part of the minister's dress, his books, &c.; and a respectable peasant as an attendant on the general cavalcade. I will not detain you by particulars, which, however interesting, would draw me too far from the main object of my attention. I will only say, that the appearance of the congregation, their neat and becoming costume, their order, and their seriousness, together with the fervor, tenderness, and simplicity, with which the good minister addressed them, both in his sermon n the morning, and his catechetical lecture in the afternoon, conveyed to my mind the most delightful impression—that of a sincere and elevated devotion. The interval between the services was passed partly in dining at the house of the happy bourgeois, (for the duty of fetching and entertaining their pastor, is, in the estimation of these simple people, a privilege of the highest order,) and partly in visiting some of the excellent individuals, both men and women, particularly the latter, in which this part of the parish abounds. The affability and graceful condescension with which the pastor saluted every member of his flock, wherever he met them, and the affectionate reverence with which young and old returned the salutation, were peculiarly pleasing: it was, on both sides, if a ceremony at all, the ceremony of the heart. On our return to the parsonage, the evening was passed in edifying conversation, and concluded by a French hymn, in which all the household united. On the ensuing morning, I had the honor of conveying my venerable host, amidst the bowings of his parishioners, who gazed with wonder at the unusual sight of their stationary pastor seated in a travelling carriage, to the house of Messrs. Legrand, at Foudai, another of the villages in this extensive parish. Here we breakfasted; and, after much pleasing conversation with this amiable, benevolent, and well-informed family, I had the high honor of being introduced to Sophia Bernard, and Catharine Scheidecker!!! Maria Schepler, the second on the list of this memorable trio, had, I found, been removed to her rest: the two whom I have mentioned, and who now stood before me, remaine to fill up the measure of their usefulness in the work of their Lord. Never shall I forget the manner in which these interesting peasants received me, when, addressing them by name, I told them that I had known them nearly fourteen years, and that the account of their services, communicated to us by the pastor whom they so greatly assisted, had been instrumental in stirring up the zeal of many to labor after their example. 'Oh, Sir,' said Sophia Bernard, the tears filling her eyes at the time, 'this does indeed humble us;' adding many pious remarks in relation to their obscurity, the imperfection of their works, and the honor they considered it to labor for Him who had done so much, yea, every thing, for them. The scene was truly affecting. It was not without many an effort that I tore myself from it, and hurried from the Ban de la Roche, that seat of simplicity, piety, and true Christian refinement, to resume my journey along the beaten road, and to pursue my object among scenes, which, whatever pleasures I had to expect, would suffer in the comparison with those which I had left behind me."

In most of his religious tenets, Oberlin was strictly orthodox and evangelical. The main doctrine that seemed to occupy his whole mind, was that God was his Father. "*Our* Father," as he would not unfrequently say, "and thus we may *always* feel Him." The doctrine of sanctification also held a high place in his creed, though, in his discourses, he principally dwelt upon the freeness of the Gospel, the willingness of Christ to receive all who come to him in sincerity of heart, the blessed efficacy of prayer and the absolute necessity of divine grace.

It may here be considered necessary, for the sake of biographical faithfulness, to observe that upon some points he certainly held very fanciful and unwarranted notions, more particularly upon those relative to a future state. In the interpretation of John 14: 2, for example, ("In my Father's house are many mansions,) he considered that there was an exact relation between our state here and the very mansion we should enter hereafter; and this relation, or proportion of happiness, he seemed to himself to have so accurately ascertained, by the help of types drawn from the different parts of the Temple, beginning with the outer court of the sanctuary and ending with the Holy of Holies, and from expressions denoting the state of the redeemed in the Book of Revelations, as to be able to draw a map of the other world; and this map he printed and hung up in his church. He also held the doctrine of an intermediate state, which he supposed to be one of continual improvement, and likewise believed that we shall become progressively holy in heaven. He seemed to hope that the passage 1 Cor. 15: 28, where it is said that "all things" shall be subjected unto the Almighty, and the Son also himself shall be subjected, "that God may be all in all," might include not only the little flock of Christ's immediate followers, but, ultimately, at some almost indefinite period, through the boundless mercy of God, and the blood of Jesus, which was shed for the sins of the *whole* world, all the race of mankind. And he was strengthened in this belief by understanding in another than the ordinary sense, that as in Adam all die, even sc in Christ shall *all* be made alive. It is needless to say of these doctrines that they are fanciful and mistaken, and not to be defended by an accurate application of Scripture. But, whatever hold they had upon Oberlin's mind, they appeared very little in his preaching, and did not at all interfere with the plainest statement of the doctrine of justification by faith in the merits of our Redeemer, and sanctification by his Spirit, and of the absolute necessity of both the one and the other to meetness for the heavenly inheritance.

Oberlin was accustomed to preach very alarmingly on the judgment to come, and the punishment of the wicked; though, at the same time, he held out the fatherly love of God to every returning sinner, who would seek Him through Jesus Christ. These last mentioned doctrines may be said to have constituted the leading features of his ministry. He had a remarkable reverence for the Bible, and especially for the Books of Moses, and the Gospels. He was led to adopt many of the laws of Moses, because, he said, although the ceremonial law is rejected, the object of that law, the glory of God and the good of man, remains, and therefore the law itself ought to be retained. The subjoined note marks a number of passages from the laws of Moses, which Oberlin adopted, and which he applied with great force and interest in his own conduct, and in his instructions to his people.*

---

* *Alms.* Deut. 14 : 28, &c. 15 : 7. Mat. 3 : 10.

Prevention of dangers. Deut. 22 : 8. Exod. 21 : 33.

Strangers. Exod. 22 : 21. 23 : 9. Lev. 19 : 33, 34. 24 : 22. Num. 15 : 14. Deut. 10 : 18, 19. 24 : 14, 19. 26 : 12. 27 : 19.

Also for Strangers. Exod. 12 : 19. Num. 9 : 14.

Solomon appointed a court for Strangers: 2 Chron. 6 : 32. This court the avarice of the Jews suffered to become a market, and from this market Jesus drove the buyers and sellers.

Fertility. To make a country fertile, it must be

It may, indeed, be doubted whether there was not much in the history of Moses, as well as in his law, which remarkably adapted itself to Oberlin's experience and views.

This coincidence has been pointed out to me by the Rev. Francis Cunningham, who visited the Ban de la Roche in 1820, when Oberlin was in the eightieth year of his age. He thus writes

"In contemplating the history and circumstances of this venerable man, I could not but call to mind that of the Patriarch, whose law, as well as example, he seems so attentively to have followed. Oberlin, like Moses, was trained to another service than that which he was ultimately called to follow. He had to civilize, as well as to instruct, a people degraded by long habits, deeply rooted, and which sprung from wretchedness and poverty. Like Moses, he was a great lover of order, and had a singular tact for government. Like him too, he united remarkable meekness with occasional impetuosity, and the truest decision of character. As of Moses at the end of his pilgrimage, so it may be said of Oberlin, his eye

---

guarded from bad seasons, dearth and famine. Lev. 26: 3, 14. Deut. 11: 13, 16. Mal. 3: 10.

Politeness. Rom. 12: 10. 1 Cor. 13: 4, 5.

To protect ourselves from the evil of war. Lev. 25: 18, 19. Deut. 33: 28, 29. Prov. 1: 33.

Doctors. Exod. 15: 26. 2 Chron. 16: 12.

Law-suit. Mat. 5: 39, 40.

First-fruits. Exod. 22: 29. Deut. 15: 19.

Payment. Lev. 19: 13. Deut. 24: 14. Jer. 22: 13. Rom. 13: 8. Mat. 5. 25.

Health. Exod. 15: 26. Mal. 4: 2.

Prolonged life. Deut. 4: 40. 5: 32, 33. 6: 2. 11: 9. 17: 20. 30: 17, 18. 30: 20. 32: 46, 47.

was scarcely dim, and his natural force was hardly abated. They each lived to testify of a people following the ways of God, (Deut. 33 : 29) 'Happy art thou, O Israel; who is like unto thee, O people saved by the Lord;' and now as they fought the same fight, passed through the same tribulation, and washed their robes and made them white in the blood of the Lamb, they dwell together before the throne of God, and serve him day and night in his temple; they have entered into the same joy, and are crowned with the same reward. For there, this most holy, most devoted, and most useful man, has now opened his eyes to receive the recompense of his faith, his patience, and his labors:—and there, as one who hath turned many to righteousness, he will shine in the crown of his Redeemer for ever and ever."

In his sermons, Oberlin was simple, energetic, and affectionate, continually speaking to his people under the appellation of "my dear friends." He appeared to study a *colloquial* plainness, interspersing his discourses with *images* and allusions, which, had they been addressed to a more refined audience, might have been deemed homely, but which were particularly adapted to the capacities and wants of his secluded villagers. He would frequently introduce biographical anecdotes of persons distinguished for their piety; and the boundless field of nature furnished him with striking illustrations to explain spiritual things. But the *Bible* itself, "the dear Bible," as he exclaimed with tears of gratitude a short time before his last illness, was the grand source of all his instructions. It formed the study of his life, and, as he said, constituted his only consolation under all trials, the source of his strength, and the ruling principle of his actions:—how, then, could he do less than recommend it to others? He was in the habit of citing very largely from it, from the conviction that the simple exposition of the Word of God was the best means of efficaciously interesting his flock. His sermons were almost always composed with the greatest care: and when unable, for want of time, to write them out at length, he made at least a tolerably full outline. In general, he committed them scrupulously to memory, but in the pulpit he did not confine himself to the precise words, and would indeed sometimes change the subject altogether, if he saw that another was apparently better suited to the circumstances of his auditory.

The following extracts, taken from the notes of some of his autograph sermons, are characteristic of that originality and devotedness which formed one of their distinguishing features.

The first was preached in the parish church of Waldbach the very day after his son Henry's death. Some account of that beloved son has been inserted in a previous part of this Memoir, and it may there be seen that the chief comfort which he experienced in his last moments, was derived from the words which his father took for his text, "From death unto life."

"*Nov.* 16, 1817.

("The day after the death of my son, Henry Gottfried.)

"Verily, verily, I say unto you, He that heareth my word, and believeth on him that sent me, hath everlasting life, and shall not come into condemnation; but is passed from death unto life." John 5:24. last clause.

"From death unto life! From death unto life! That is the device, the motto, the rallying-word of Christians, that is, of all those persons who have faithfully guarded their covenant of Baptism. And of all the persons who, though fallen from he grace of God, repent sincerely, remembering with sorrow their infringement of the covenant of Baptism, and the violation of their covenant renewed at the time of their confirmation—who are returned to the Savior of our souls, and have aspired to the honor and the happiness of living before him, with him, and for him.

"From death unto life! Ah, what a serene prospect in regard to the future! What joyous hope, what delicious tints does it shed upon all parts of their life here below! upon all the crosses, upon all the paths sprinkled with tears; when one has a lively feeling of the efficacy of this word of the apostle of the Lord:—"All things work together for good, to them that love God," *all*, all things, sad or joyous, sweet or bitter, and tribulations even the most grievous, "all things" contribute to their true good, to their happiness and eternal prosperity.

"They are *all*, and especially the more bitter—they are *all*, the steps which God uses to lead us from one degree of divine virtue to another—always tending to more perfection in faith and confidence in God, in filial and cheerful obedience to his commandments—in humility, sweetness, gentleness, delicacy, in sentiment, taste, beneficence, in charity, purity, in a word, in all the celestial virtues.

"But in advancing the Christian in virtue, it advances him in resemblance to God, in the re-establishment of the divine image, and consequently always to greater brightness in the regions of light, always to greater nearness to the residence of God, our Creator and Father. For to each one shall be assigned a dwelling more or less great in glory, more or less near to the inexhaustible source of all felicity, according to h greater or less resemblance, internal, spiritual an moral, to our God.

"From death unto life! Ah, how, by this hope, when it is well founded, the idea of death, otherwise so terrific, loses its terror, in proportion as one is right in his expectation of this ravishing change! When we are born, we enter upon death:—for it is thus that our Creator and Father has constituted and described our present life—poor, pretended life,—life full of thorns, of sufferings, and of tears. God has called it death, and so it is; since men are fallen from their glorious primitive state—since they have detached their hearts from God by attaching them to that which is transitory and perishable—since they have forsaken the fountain of living waters, and hewed them out cisterns, broken cisterns, that can hold no water, or a water that is salt, offensive, infected and poisonous.

"But when we open our hearts to the voice of the Divine Shepherd, who calls us so often to himself; when we aspire to the incomparable honor and happiness of being received into the number of his sheep: ah, what a change is then made in us!—how from being worldly-minded do we become heavenly! how then is the image of God re-established in us!

"Then the aim of our actions, and the scope,

and the design of our enterprises become altogether different from what they were before. Ah! it is no more then to become rich, and to gain those advantages which are transient and perishable, that we desire, long for, aspire to, in our labors and our savings. Oh, no! In the union of our hearts and of our sentiments with the Lord Jesus Christ, we espouse his interests, we seek to aid even himself in his great work, in delivering the poor human family from all its innumerable evils of mind and body, from all its frightful moral corruption, and from all the innumerable species of sufferings which are in its train.

"That is the aim which animates Christians, the disciples of the Lord Jesus, and for such, Death, the king of terrors, loses that which renders him most formidable. By these considerations they become indifferent as to living or dying.

"Do they dwell long upon the earth?—it is for glorifying the Lord as much as they are able, following their vocation, and serving him in his great work.

"Are they recalled from this earth by death?—it is for continuing to serve him in his great work, and to labor that the name of God be glorified, that his kingdom may find access everywhere, and that all the world may take pleasure in doing his will.

"For this reason St. Paul would not concern himself to choose between life and death—between remaining longer in this world or going to the other. He declared that his desire would be rather to depart and be with Christ, but in reference to those persons who by his means had been converted to the Lord, it might be more necessary that he should remain still in this lower life, for his aim was, that the Lord might be glorified by him whether in this world or in the other. Phil. 1 : 20, 24.

"And, 2 Cor. 5 : 15, he said; The Lord Jesus died for all, that they which live should not henceforth live to themselves, but to him who died for them.

"And, Rom. 14 : 7, 8. None of us (his disciples) liveth to himself, and none of us dieth to himself. But whether we live (in this world) we live to the Lord; or whether we die, we die to the Lord: whether then we live or we die, we are always the Lord's.

"Ah, dear friends! may the consideration of such a life, may the contemplation of that country on the other side of death, ever be pleasant and attractive!

"May we be able, when dying, to sing in heart these verses of Drelincourt.

I.

Oh welcome sweet day, long so fondly desir'd,
When my holy Redeemer would gather my soul;
My heart springs to meet him—Roll on, minutes, roll,
Till I mount to those mansions to which I aspir'd.

II.

Sweet moment—brought near me so long by faith's eye,
Thou hast come to cut short the dark thread of my woes;
Oh Jesus, in whom I believe and repose,
Exalt me from earth, where I liv'd but to sigh.

III.

Oh God, earth is cover'd with dangers and snares—
Earth is full of transgressions, and errors and cares—
Her pleasures possess not one charm to my eyes,
As the runner, whose soul is intent on his prize,

Mortality now to thy hands I resign,
My soul will be full when thy glory is mine!"

Then follow the notes containing the particulars of Henry's death, which seemed to introduce the personal subject, if it were introduced at all. But it is the more probable that it was not, as the calamity was so recent, and so deeply affecting to his father.

The remarkable affection that existed between the venerable pastor and his son, has been before alluded to. But in this sermon we have a proof that whilst he felt for the loss of his child, he could not forget for a moment the state of those before whom he was preaching, and upon whose account he desired to make this occasion one of unusual profit as well as interest.

Oberlin, as I have stated above, was fond of drawing analogies between the natural and spiritual world. The following extracts from a sermon preached on a week day (November 16, 1819) will illustrate the manner in which he did so. It also bears some marks of his peculiarities of view as to a future state:—

"The children of this world marry and are given in marriage.

"But they which shall be counted worthy to obtain that world and the resurrection from the dead, neither marry nor are given in marriage, neither can they die any more, for they are equal unto the Angels, and are the children of God, being the children of the resurrection."

"The Lord presents us here at a glance, a futurity highly transporting for any one who has not a concern more grand and pressing than that of becoming a true disciple of Jesus Christ, a true member of his body. To comprehend this beautiful passage, we must explain certain terms.

"1. What does the Lord intend by "this world," and by "that to come?"

"By this world the Lord understands the actual state of the human race, since it has fallen from its first glorious estate.

"By the world to come, he understands, the state, marvellously glorious, of those in whom God shall have perfectly re-established his image, and the former glorious state for which we had been created.

"2. What does the Lord understand by being "children of the resurrection?" It is not the general awakening of the dead at the last day, to prepare them to appear before the tribunal of the Supreme Judge. But it is that perfect deliverance from all the evils that sin has brought upon us, and the re-establishment of the primitive glory. This is what the Lord intends by "children of the resurrection."

"3. Who are they who shall be esteemed worthy of this glorious resurrection, and of the perfect re-establishment of the image of God?

"Those who give themselves, heart, soul, and spirit, to the Lord Jesus Christ, and strive to enter in at the strait gate, and who, to this end, study and keep diligently all that the Lord ha commanded his disciples—who by continua prayer from the bottom of their hearts, and frequent use of the Lord's supper, endeavor to be always more and more closely united to the Lord—who aspire to love God with all their heart, with all their soul, with all their strength, and with all their mind—and to love their neighbor truly as themselves, and to be faithful man-servants and maid-servants of God in his vineyard.

"Those who labor to obtain these graces, not only for themselves, but also for their families, and their friends, and their acquaintances, as far as they can reach by their prayers.

"When such persons, by their faith, humility, zeal and charity, have passed through the different lower heavens, and shall have arrived at perfect holiness, the perfection of the saints complete in righteousness, and shall be admitted into the class and rank of dwellers on mount Zion or the kingdom of heaven, then they shall receive their glorified body, or "the resurrection" of which our Lord here speaks.

"4. Then they shall not die any more; or as the Lord expresses it in the Revelations by John, chap. 21 : 4. 'and there shall be no more death, neither sorrow, nor crying, neither shall there be any more pain: for the former things are passed away.'

"Ye know, dear friends! that all terrestrial nature is a representation of the spiritual. The caterpillar, and all insects, pass through different states which bear no resemblance to one another. At first, issuing from the egg, they are only diminutive worms; in time they strip off their outer skin, and go forth as it were in a new form: but finally they receive a form entirely new, that of the chrysalis. This is, in a manner, a new animal, different from the first in its figure and properties. But this is not all. Under the form of this chrysalis, it is prepared to become another new animal, entirely more perfect than in its two former states—it is now the butterfly, ornamented with beautiful colors, and having tastes and properties completely different.

"Now he disdains the gross nourishment of his first condition, and takes that which is more pure and more perfect, the honey of the flowers. As to his movements, he has now no longer need of his feet to transport him from place to place: by means of his wings, he gaily lifts himself, and quickly darts over walls, rivers, and mountains.

"In like manner, those who are in Jesus Christ, pass, according to the degree of their advancement in humility, charity, holiness—they pass, by different changes of their bodies, internal, spiritual, visible only to angels, but hidden to us in terrestrial bodies. And these changes from brightness to brightness, "from glory to glory," continue until their bodies are fashioned and are like to the glorious body of the Lord Jesus Christ.

"Ah, dear friends! what a ravishing prospect —what astonishing and delicious hope—O! let us ever animate ourselves to pursue in Jesus Christ our sanctification, and tighten the bonds of our union with him. It is by him, the dear Lord—it is only by him, that any attains to all this—for he it is, whom God hath given unto us to find in him wisdom, righteousness, sanctification, and glorious redemption and salvation." 1 Cor. 1: 30.

Oberlin always concluded the Sabbath afternoon's service with *catechetical* exercises; and as this was intended more particularly for the benefit of the children, he endeavored to render his afternoon's discourse even more simple than that of the morning had been, and to adapt his language to the age of his younger hearers.

'My friends," said he, upon one of these occasions, wishing to give them, if possible, some idea of eternity, "If a single grain of sand were brought into this room once every hundred years, many centuries must elapse before the floor could be covered. That moment would, however, arrive; but, even when it came, the spirits of the blessed would be still in the enjoyment of heavenly happiness, for they are immortal; and if a grain of sand were to be brought at the same stated interval for many thousands of centuries, until the room were entirely filled, those happy beings would still be immortal, and eternity would be as boundless as when the first grain was brought."

"The good pastor," says Mr. Steinkopff, from whose journal the editor has been kindly allowed to make the following extracts, "considers his flock as his own children, and they look up to him with the most profound respect and veneration. I never witnessed so delightfully affecting a scene as the church of Waldbach, quite full, apparently, of attentive people. It stands very near the parsonage, and is plain, neat, and clean, with a gallery all round. When we were there, on the 11th of June, 1820, it was completely filled with peasants in the costume of the country, and there was not a countenance among them that indicated indifference; the greater part evinced the utmost seriousness and attention. When the reverend pastor entered, all stood up; he placed himself before the communion table; it was plain, covered with a white cloth, fringed all round. He first gave out a hymn. When it was sung, he read a prayer from the ritual, during which all knelt, and covered their faces. He then gave out another hymn; after which he went to one part of the church where the children sat, and called over their names, to *see* if any were absent. Then all knelt down again whilst he prayed; then they sung, and he went into the pulpit and gave out his text, after another prayer 'He shall see of the travail of his soul, and shall be satisfied.' Isa. 53 : 11. He spoke in the plainest and most familiar manner; mentioned the errors of the times, against which he warned his hearers, particularly dwelling on the importance of sanctification. 'Those who give themselves up to intemperance,' said he, 'and to the enjoyment of luxuries, without concerning themselves about their poorer brethren, and yet think that with all this they shall go to heaven, because Christ died for sinners, are mistaken. No: the Gospel says quite otherwise. We must deny ourselves, lay aside our sins, lead a holy and godly life, and then our Blessed Redeemer will save us.' He earnestly warned them against sin. Not a sound was to be heard. Every countenance expressed attention. When he had finished, he read some verses of a hymn expressive of entire devotedness to God. 'My dear friends,' said he, 'may these be the feelings of our hearts, and as such let us sing them. They then sang them with deep interest.

The following is a translation:—

"O Lord, thy heavenly grace impart,
And fix my frail inconstant heart.
Henceforth my chief desires shall be,
To dedicate myself to Thee!
To Thee, my God, to Thee!

"Whate'er pursuits my time employ,
One thought shall fill my soul with joy;
That silent, secret thought shall be,
That all my hopes are fix'd on Thee—
On Thee, my God, on Thee!

"Thy glorious eye pervadeth space,
Thou'rt present, Lord, in every place,
And, wheresoe'er my lot may be,
Still shall my spirit cleave to Thee—
To Thee, my God, to Thee!

"Renouncing every worldly thing,
Safe 'neath the covert of thy wing,
My sweetest thought henceforth shall be,
That all I want I find in Thee,
In Thee, my God, in Thee!

"Two children were then brought to be baptized; after which he pronounced the blessing. Whilst the people were going out of church, another verse was sung. Those nearest the door went out first, all in order and in silence. There are two doors in the church; the pulpit is placed in the middle, next the back, so that the congregation is in front, down each side. Before it stands the communion table. All are seated on benches. There are, against the gallery, half a dozen pictures; one is of our Savior on the cross."

Dr. Steinkopff writes the following letter, descriptive of the same interesting scene.

"*Waldbach, in the Steinthal,*
June 12, 1820.

"I cannot describe the veneration I felt on approaching Mr. Oberlin, that servant of God, and benefactor of man, who, in his eightieth year, is still full of health, vigor, and activity, and gladly spends his remaining strength in doing good. Serenity and cheerfulness are depicted on his countenance; and he delights in communicating to his Christian friends something of that peace of God which possesses his own soul.

"Yesterday I attended divine service in his church. Notwithstanding a pouring rain, it was completely filled. Mr. Oberlin's assistant in the ministerial office, (the Rev. Mr. Graff,) assured me that every house in the five villages under his pastoral care, was now provided with a Bible, and that every child who came to receive catechetical instruction brought a New Testament with him. But for the sake of those who applied from a distance, I gladly complied with his wish to furnish him and his son, at Rothau, with one hundred and twenty German Bibles and Testaments. After divine service, three Catholic peasants applied for De Sacy's Testament. One paid three francs for a copy. He gave Mr. Oberlin the pleasing information that many of his Catholic neighbors had already procured the New Testament, and were in the constant habit of reading it. Mr. Oberlin's son, who lives on the most friendly terms with the Catholic priest, lately presented his schoolmaster with a copy.

"I accompanied the venerable patriarch in some of his pastoral visits. Wherever he went, respect and affection met him. The children hailed his appearance. They immediately produced their Bibles, or Testaments, read to him, or listened to his truly paternal exhortations and admonitions."

Every Friday Oberlin conducted a service in German, for the benefit of those inhabitants of the vicinity to whom that language was more familiar than French. His congregation on a Sunday consisted, on an average, of six hundred persons, but on a Friday of two hundred; and Oberlin, laying aside all form, seemed on such occasions more like a grandfather surrounded by his children and grandchildren, to whom he was giving suitable admonition and instruction, than the minister of an extensive parish. In order that no time might be lost, he used to make his female hearers knit stockings, during the service, not indeed for themselves or their families, but for their poorer neighbors, as he believed that this charitable employment need not distract their attention, or interrupt that devotional spirit which generally pervaded the Friday evening assemblies. When he had pursued for half an hour the train of his reflections upon the portion of Scripture which he had just been reading, he would often say to them, "Well, my children, are you not tired?—Have you not had enough?—Tell me, my friends." To which inquiry his parishioners would generally reply, "No, papa, go on;—we should like to hear a little more," though on some occasions, with characteristic frankness, the answer was "Enough, we think, for the present;" and the good old man would leave off in the midst of his discourse, or wait a little, and presently resume it, putting the same question again at intervals, until he saw that the attention of his congregation began to flag, or until they, perceiving that he spoke with less ease, would thank him for the things he had said, and beg him to conclude.

Such was the general esteem in which he was

held, that Catholics as well as Protestants were fond of attending his preaching. The following conversation took place between an English gentleman and the driver of the car in which it was found necessary to proceed from Schirmeck to Waldbach; no apology can be deemed necessary for introducing it, in illustration of the respect in which Oberlin was universally regarded by the peasantry.

"You are going then, Sirs, to see our good pastor Oberlin," said the latter.

"Yes, we are going to see him. Do you know him?"

"Do I know him!" continued the man, "yes, I know him well. I have heard him preach many a time."

"But you are a Catholic, are you not?"

"Yes, we are Catholics, we are of Schirmeck; yet this does not hinder us from hearing the good pastor of Waldbach sometimes."

"Do you find that he preaches well?"

"O yes. I esteem him much. He often makes us all rain the warm tears."

The honest charioteer spoke a very intelligible French, quite distinct from the *patois* of Schirmeck; and this circumstance, together with a certain touch of military *sang froid* in his manner, not entirely concealed by his fustian jacket, prompted the inquiry whether he had served under Napoleon.

"Yes, Sir, you are right," replied he, "I have been a soldier. When one is a soldier, it is easy to contract bad habits."

"For all that, I have found one contracts them easily enough anywhere."

"It may be," said the man. "For myself, I tell you frankly that I was not better than others; and when I come to hear pastor Oberlin preach, he makes me very much think that I am not any too good now. He is right, the pastor is right; for it is true, very true."

"Yes; but do you not think that *this* is a truth very necessary to be learned? Do you not believe that he who shows us our faults, is one of our best friends."

"Yes: for in order to be healed, one must know his malady."

"Certainly! You are then highly favored in having a minister who makes you feel the truth."

"You are right. And I assure you that he is a man who endeavors to be of use to us in every possible way."

"Tell me now what he has done."

"What he has done! He has done every thing that could be done. See;—he has done every thing. In the first place, this road here,—he made it for us."

"Ah,—but it is not absolutely the best in the world."

"That may be; but see, Sir, it has not been many years since we would not pass it with a little car like this. The pastor has superintended the work upon all this road; he has even labored with his own hands, to encourage others."

"And that little bridge there, that we are going to cross?"

"Yes, indeed, and that bridge too;—he caused it to be made."

"He must be rich, to do all these things."

"One might say both *yes* and *no*."

"How?"

"One might say *yes;* because if he had all that he has given away to others, he would be very rich. And one may say *no*, because he lays up nothing,—absolutely nothing; he gives *all* to the poor;—all, Sir, all. You are going to see his house. You need not think to find it very elegant."

But to return to Oberlin himself.

One of his prevailing desires was that all, to whatever class or denomination they might belong, whilst conscientiously adhering to their own peculiar creeds, should grow in an acquaintance with those common truths which constitute the essence of the Gospel. "Are you a Christian?" said he to a Catholic gentleman, who visited the Ban de la Roche in the autumn of 1820;—"if you are a Christian, my dear friend, we are of the same religion. If you believe in the utter depravity of human nature, in the necessity of repentance, and whilst adoring God, pray to Him to crown your efforts to become better, we are of the same religion. Follow the law traced by the dear Savior; it only is the true law. All the forms and ceremonies that different sects have added to this law are of little importance."

Perceiving that the eyes of his visitor were directed to a portrait of Luther that hung against the wall of his study, "That man has been,' said he, "like every founder of a sect, much applauded and much calumniated. And if you will promise me not to be offended," continued he smiling, "I will tell you something about him. The popes, for a long time, arrogated to themselves temporal powers and privileges, in a very different spirit from that spirit of humility by which the first followers of Jesus Christ were distinguished. Taking advantage of the credulity of the people, they extended their dominion over nearly the whole of Europe; Turkey alone being free from their sway. Leo X. wished to unite the Christian princes against this latter kingdom, but it was necessary to obtain money, in order to secure their co-operation. Leo, who was remarkable for the patronage he afforded to the fine arts, was also in want of funds to finish the famous cathedral of St. Peter. He devised the plan of selling indulgences. These were notes payable at sight, for the enfranchisement of souls in purgatory; a place never mentioned by Jesus Christ and his apostles. Depôts of them were opened in the priests' houses, in the monasteries, and even in the public houses. The priests were employed in persuading the people to purchase them. An Augustine monk, the son of a blacksmith, of Eisleben, was led to consider what power these indulgences could possibly possess, and ascending the pulpit, after a priest who had been inculcating these doctrines, he excited in the minds of his hearers the indignation with which his own was filled. This Augustine, whose name was Martin Luther, proceeded to apply to several princes, some of whom espoused his cause. He spread the doctrines of the Reformation; abolished those of the monks; and, taking Scripture for his guide, returned to the simple communion of bread and wine; he denied the power of baptism to take away original sin; condemned auricular confession; and declared that popes and councils had no authority to add any thing to the religion of Jesus Christ and his apostles, seeing that if Jesus Christ had wished his religion to be different from that which he taught, he would himself have delivered it differently. Luther opened the way for a great revolution, and violent means were taken to oppose his proceedings. I will add no more," continued he, "I only wished to mention the causes and the principal effects of the Reformation. Luther was not the founder of a new religion; he only brought us back to the religion of Jesus Christ. God will regard all who adhere to the doctrines of his divine Son with equal favor, be they Catholics or Lutherans."

The following anecdotes are illustrative of the paternal influence which Oberlin exercised over his flock, as well as of his readiness to assist those who differed from him in their religious tenets. A young woman of Schirmeck, of the Roman Catholic persuasion, had married a Protestant of Waldbach. This man had enemies; he was, comparatively speaking, rich, and his fortune might possibly have some connexion with the motives of their animosity. The young woman became the mother of a little girl, who, by mutual consent, and in pursuance of the marriage agreement, was to be brought up in the religion of the former, and baptized by the clergyman of Schirmeck. To repair thither it was necessary to take the road over the mountains; but, at the moment of their setting off, they were informed that the enemies of the husband had laid a scheme to waylay them at a particular turn of the road, to spring out upon him when he reached it, and to compel him by menaces and ill-treatment to consent to their unjust demands.

Their journey could not very well be delayed, as the priest had been informed of their intended arrival; and yet they were afraid to undertake it, on account of the impending danger. In this painful dilemma they went to consult Oberlin. He, after exhorting them to place their trust in God, most kindly offered to accompany them, to render his aid and protection should they require it. On arriving at a spot in the forest where there was reason to fear an ambuscade, Oberlin knelt down, and, extending his hands over the young people, exclaimed with a loud voice, "Great God! Thou seest wickedness lying in wait, and conspiring mischief. Thou seest innocence in alarm. Almighty God! avert the danger, or give thy children strength to surmount it."

At this moment several men, who had been concealed behind a thicket of beech trees, discovered themselves, and rushed forwards, uttering the most threatening exclamations. Oberlin took the little infant in his arms, and advanced towards them with a calmness which did not conceal his indignation, yet still left room for the hope of pardon. "There," said he to them, "is the babe which has done you so much injury—which disturbs the peace of your days." Dismayed at the presence of their pastor, whom they little expected to meet with in the character of an escort to persons going to perform a Roman Catholic ceremony, and finding from the few words which he had addressed to them that he was not ignorant of their bad designs, they did not attempt to dissimulate, but, confessing their crime, begged pardon of the young man, and offered terms of reconciliation. Thus providentially rescued from the danger which had threatened them, the young people continued their walk to Schirmeck, while Oberlin returned to Waldbach with the men whom he had thus prevented from doing evil. When they reached the entrance of the village, "My children," said he as he left them, "remember the day on the moun tains, if you wish that I should forget it."

Another morning (in the early part of his ministry,) as Oberlin was at work in his study he heard a great noise in the village. Rushing out, he perceived a foreigner whom almost the whole population were loading with abusive and threatening language. "A Jew! a Jew!" resounded on all sides, as the good pastor forced his way through the crowd; and it was with difficulty that he could obtain silence. As soon, however, as he could make himself heard, he rebuked them with great warmth for having proved themselves unworthy the name of Christians by treating the unfortunate stranger in so cruel a manner. He added, that if this poor man wanted the *name* of a Christian, they wanted the *spirit* of Christians. The same enlargement of mind distinguished Oberlin on all occasions. And whatever men might say, he still remembered the Apostle's injunction, Gal. 6: 10. "Let us do good unto all men."

I shall conclude this chapter respecting Ober lin's private and ministerial character, with the following questions which he addressed to his flock in writing, requiring from them satisfactory replies to each inquiry. They prove that his solicitude for their welfare descended to the smallest details, both with respect to their temporal and spiritual concerns, and that he neglected nothing to which he thought it his duty to call their attention.

Questions addressed by Pastor Oberlin to his Parishioners.

1. Do you, and your family, regularly attend places of religious instruction?

2. Do you never pass a Sunday without employing yourself in some charitable work?

3. Do neither you, nor your wife or children, ever wander in the woods on a Sunday, in search of wild raspberries, strawberries, whortleberries, mulberries, or hazel-nuts, instead of going to church?—and, if you have erred in this manner, will you solemnly promise to do so no more?

4. Are you careful to provide yourself with clean and suitable clothes for going to church in on the Sunday?*

5. Do those who are provided with necessary clothes employ a regular part of their income to procure them for their destitute neighbors, or to relieve their other necessities?

6. Have your civil and ecclesiastical overseers reason to be satisfied with your conduct, and that of the other members of your family?

7. Do you so love and reverence our Lord and Savior, Jesus Christ, as to feel united in the bonds of Christian fellowship with that flock of which he is the Pastor?

* During the first years of Oberlin's residence in the Ban de la Roche, the inhabitants were so miserably off for wearing apparel that they could only go to church by turns, being obliged to borrow each other's clothes in order to appear decently attired.

8. Do the animals which belong to you cause no injury or inconvenience to others?—(Guard against this, for it would be as fire in tow, and a source of mutual vexation.)

9. Do you give your creditors reason to be satisfied with your honesty and punctuality?—or can they say of you that you are more desirou of purchasing superfluous clothes than of dis charging your debts?

10. Have you paid all that is due this quarter to the churchwarden, schoolmaster and shepherd?

11. Do you punctually contribute your share towards the repairing of the roads?*

---

* That Oberlin considered the repairing of roads as a religious duty incumbent upon all his parishioners, (since it conduced to the public good,) appears from the following curious and characteristic letter, which he addressed to them Nov. 9, 1804.

"Road between Foudai and Zolbach.

"Dear friends of Foudai!

"Several persons at Zolbach have long been desirous that a certain road in your district, which runs towards Zolbach, should be mended and put into repair.

"Such a measure would tend greatly to the advantage of Foudai. But for whose sake will you do it? Will you do it from love to your Heavenly Father, to whom you pray every day, and whom in the Lord's Prayer you call Father, and who requires you to prove your faith by you works? Will you do it from love to the Lord Jesu Christ, who, during his stay upon earth, went about doing good, and who has redeemed us in order to make to himself a peculiar people zealous of good works? Will you do it from love to God's children who are at Zolbach?—you know that all the services which you render to the children of God, and the followers of Jesus Christ, God regards as done to himself. Will you do it from love to

12. Have you, in order to contribute to the general good, planted upon the common at least twice as many trees as there are heads in your family?

13. Have you planted them properly, or only as idle and ignorant people would do, to save hemselves trouble?

14. When the magistrate wishes to assemble the commonalty, do you always assist him as far as lies in your power; and, if it be impossible for you to attend yourself, are you careful to inform him of your absence, and to assign a proper reason for it?

15. Do you send your children regularly to school?

16. Do you watch over them as God requires you should do? And is your conduct towards them, as well as your wife's, such as will insure their affection, respect, and obedience?

17. Are you frugal in the use of wood? And do you contrive to make your fires in as economical a manner as possible?

18. Do you keep a dog unless there be absolute necessity?

19. Have you proper drains in your yard for carrying off the refuse water?

20. Are you, as well as your sons, acquainted with some little handicraft work to employ your

---

he servants of mammon who are at Zolbach, in order to set them a good example, and to win their affections by your kindness?—or, will you do it from compassion to the animals which your Heavenly Father has created, and which he has himself honored by his covenant with Noah after the deluge, Gen. 9: 9?"

spare moments, instead of letting them pass away in idleness?

With regard to the purport of the fifth question, as Oberlin was most particular in devoting a certain share of his own income to the alleviation of the wants of others, and in accustoming himself to the strictest self-denial in order to increase his means of doing good, so he used his utmost endeavors to persuade others to imitate his example, and to avoid any superfluity in their clothes or manner of living, that they might be the better able to assist their poorer neighbors.

He addressed the following advice to the mothers in his parish, on observing that it was becoming a prevalent fashion amongst them to put cambric frills to their little boys' shirts—an extravagance which he deemed extremely reprehensible:

"Various mothers are, I observe, beginning to put frills of muslin or of cambric to their children's shirts. Do not do so, dear friends. Unpick them, cut them off, and seek not to increase the vanity of your children, which is already naturally too great. Cut off all the finery that does not correspond with your station in life, and employ yourselves in clothing the poor families of this extensive parish; many of whom are in an extremely miserable condition.

"Love your neighbors as yourselves. Renounce every superfluity, that you may be the better able to procure necessaries for those who are in want. Be their care-takers—their fathers and their mothers—for it is for this purpose that God has blessed you with more temporal wealth than he has done them. Be merciful. The time may come when you yourselves will stand in need of the mercy of God."

The following note bears also the same import: its superscription is,

" *Surplus of Hay.*"

" *Waldbach, March* 13, 1803.

" Dear Friends,

" Is not this one of the two principal commandments—'Thou shalt love thy neighbor as thyself?' Matt. 22: 39. Is it not as much as to say, when thy cattle can spare a little of thy hay, supply those who stand in need? But as thou canst not give to all who want, choose those who are in the greatest necessity and poverty, and, from among them, select such individuals as are most earnest in obeying the commandments of Jesus Christ, and in endeavoring to work out their salvation with fear and trembling. Say to thyself, 'to such will I sell my hay,' and then let them have it at so low a price, that they may rejoice and bless God.

" And afterwards be careful to furnish them with the means of liberating themselves from the debt which they have incurred, as far as thou art able to do so.

" Be the father of the poor, and God will be thy father. Remember that it is impossible to love God with thy whole heart, without loving thy neighbor also.

" Tread not in the steps of others, but be thou a follower of the Lord Jesus Christ. Be the father of the poor. Choose those who fear God most. Make good speed about it, for perhaps thou wilt not be much longer in possession of terrestrial riches."

The following little circulars, in allusion to the sixteenth question, addressed at different times by Oberlin to his parishioners, prove how constantly he endeavored to instil into their minds the necessity of bringing up their children in habits of subordination, and under their own inspection.

" *Waldbach, Feb.* 27, 1801.

" Dear Friends, Fathers and Mothers!

" I have a request to make to you. You give shepherds to your sheep, to lead them into green pastures, to feed, tend, and preserve them from danger, and you do well.

" But have you no fears for your *children?* Does not Satan go about to tempt them to do wrong? Then give them shepherds likewise, and never allow them to be left to their own devices. Let them work and amuse themselves under proper inspection and superintendence, but let this superintendence be wise, prudent, gentle, kind, and engaging, and whilst it leads you to take part in their amusements, and to direct, animate, and enliven them, let it also restrain them within due bounds. Whatever it costs you, God will restore it a thousand fold."

" *May* 29, 1803.

" 'And the Lord said unto Cain, Where is Abe thy brother? And he said, I know not; Am I my brother's keeper?' Gen. 4: 9. The Lord said to Cain, 'Where is Abel thy brother?' Oh, may these words resound continually in the ears of every parent, 'Father, where is thy *son?*'

Fathers of Belmont! Fathers of Bellefosse, of Waldbach, of Foudai, and of Zolbach! Father, where is thy son? In what village; in what house; in what company? How is he employed? It behooves you to be able to answer these inquiries by night and by day; on Sundays and on working-days; wherever you are, and whatever you are doing. You are the guardians of your children; and whether they are employed in work or in relaxation and amusement, it is your duty to superintend and direct their amusements and pursuits.

"Do it; do it, henceforth, with faithfulness, vigilance, and zeal; with earnest and secret prayer that God may pardon you for past unfaithfulness, and deliver your sons from the sin and danger into which your carelessness, and want of parental watchfulness, may have driven them. This is the desire of

"Your papa and minister,

"J. F. OBERLIN."

CHAPTER IX.

Oberlin's pastoral visits—Interview between Dr. and Mrs. Steinkopff and the Conductrice of Bellefosse—Their visit to the cottage of Madeleine Krüger; also to that of Sophia Bernard—Letter written by Mrs. C. during a visit to the Ban de la Roche in the summer of 1820—Letter from Mrs. Rauscher to the Paris Bible Society, containing an account of the death of Sophia Bernard, &c.—Amount of the sums raised at different times in Waldbach, in support of various charitable institutions.

It was not in the pulpit alone that Oberlin sought to make known the truths of the gospel; he was in the habit of paying *pastoral visits* to all the cottages in his parish; of conversing with their inhabitants on the subjects connected with their eternal welfare, and upon the various plans adopted by benevolent individuals in different parts of the world for the dissemination of religious knowledge.

In the hope of advancing their moral and spiritual welfare, he kept a book in which he made *private memoranda* respecting their various states, a task for which the insight he obtained in their respective characters, during his frequent visits, peculiarly qualified him. Amongst other heads in the book were "Idlers" and "Bad Managers. The Ten Commandments also furnished him with many distinct heads, under which he made remarks upon the state of his congregation, particularizing the conduct of such persons as he deemed reprehensible, that he might be the better able to adapt his discourses to their edification.

The affectionate manner in which he entered into familiar conversation with them upon such subjects as the diffusion of religious knowledge, the conversion of the heathen, and the exertions of God's devoted servants in bearing to others the "unsearchable riches of Christ," seldom failed to gain their attention, and to awaken in their hearts the warmest interest, whilst it had, at the same time, a most happy effect upon their manners, inducing, in some of the poor women particularly, a refinement and softness not often met with in persons of the same class, entirely free from pride, awkwardness, forwardness, or coarseness. The following anecdote is a pleasing illustration of these remarks.

During Dr. and Mrs. Steinkopff's visit to the Ban de la Roche, in 1820, they one day took a walk up the side of the mountain with Mr. Graff. The little path they were following, led to Bellefosse, whither they were going, to pay a visit to Madeleine Krüger, one of the exemplary poor women of that village. Many peasants had bowed to them as they passed, with an air of courtesy, and the women had addressed them with, "I have the honor of saluting you, Madame," making at the same time a curtsy that would not have disgraced an English drawing-room. In the middle of a wood, through which the road led, they met a peasant, simply attired, with a pleasing open countenance, and a basket at her back. "Madame," said she, addressing Mrs. Steinkopff, "I have the honor to salute you," and a most profound curtsy accompanied her words.

"Good morning! I am rejoiced to have met

you, my dear Priscilla," said Mr. Graff, returning the salutation; "I have the pleasure of introducing you to this lady and gentleman, from England. You are well acquainted with the name of the gentleman. He is Dr. Steinkopff, one of the Secretaries of the Bible Society which has supplied us with so many Bibles." "Oh, God be praised for it, my dear Sir!" replied the peasant. "Yes, I am well acquainted with your name! I have read the reports which make mention of you. Is it possible," and she joined her hands together, "that I have the honor of seeing you here on earth! Often, yes, often, I think of the people of whom I read, and who have been brought to our dear Savior, through the means, through the generosity, of that noble Society. Ah, what reason have *we* to rejoice, who live in the abundance of spiritual blessings; and how much should we wish to procure the same advantages for those who are destitute of them! Yes; we are very rich here, in this Ban de la Roche. Oh, that we may never be unfaithful to that light which God has been pleased to grant to us! I am truly delighted with all that I hear, and especially that I have the pleasure of seeing you. I recollect what our good pastor one day said at a funeral, when he saw a poor child weeping bitterly over its grandmother, whom they were going to bury: 'My dear child, instea of weeping for your grandmamma, who is now no more, endeavor to live in a manner conformable to the will of God; believe, dear, in your Savior, and then, in his good time, you will meet her again in heaven, never more to be separated.' *I* also pray, Sir, that it may please God to grant me grace to live the life of a Christian, that when I die my spirit may join those pure and happy spirits who have done so much good upon earth."

"The manners and expression of this interesting young woman," says Mrs. Steinkopff, "were very superior; for with all the animation and sprightliness of the French, much zeal and humility were conspicuous."

"On reaching Bellefosse," continues the latter, "we visited the white-washed cottage of Madeleine Krüger; its neat painted casements and clean steps announced the comfort to be found within. We entered through a kitchen, with a well furnished dresser and good oven. 'Happily come,' said she, 'you do me too much honor. I am this moment returned, and I should be sorry not to have been here on your arrival; my door is not yet unlocked;' and as she spoke she reached the key and opened it into a very good room, at one end of which stood her bed with pretty blue cotton curtains, and on one side a long table with benches around it, all as white as wood could be made; on the table lay a Moravian text-book open, in which she had been reading. Whilst we were there, a tall agreeable looking man, with a slouched hat and blue trowsers and jacket, came in; he was mayor and schoolmaster at the same time."

They afterwards proceeded to the neat, clean, and comfortable cottage of Sophia Bernard, at Foudai, with whom they were to take tea; she met them at the door and showed them into a good sized room, where, on a long deal table, al most as white as snow, were placed some beautiful flowers, and cups and saucers, cream and cakes, supplied by Mrs. Legrand, who, with her husband, sons and daughters, drank tea with them. The cups and saucers were very handsome, being of white and yellow china, and had different German sentences upon them. Upon Mrs. Steinkopff's cup this motto was inscribed, "Bete für mich, ich will für dich beten." ("Pray for me, and I will pray for thee.") Two benches were placed along the table, and Sophia stood behind, to wait. She was, like many of the female peasants of the Steinthal, delicate in her appearance, with a mild and gentle countenance, and peculiar humility of deportment. She looked upon her guests with the greatest pleasure and satisfaction, listening to all that was said, and lifting up her hands in gratitude to God, for what she heard concerning the extension of the Redeemer's kingdom on earth by the success of missionary and Bible Societies. On the departure of her visitors, she knelt down, and prayed very fervently for their protection.

The following letter, written by Mrs. C—— during her visit to the Ban de la Roche in the summer of 1820, describes the same scene, and also presents so lively and animated a picture of the venerable pastor and his family, that it cannot but be read with interest and delight.

"*Ban de la Roche, June* 7, 1820.

"My dearest ——,

* * * * *

* * * * *

My last letter from Strasbourg was written in low spirits; the sun has since shone upon us. We are now in a most uncommon and interesting spot—every thing is novel, but *the One Spirit* which acknowledges the Father, and the Son, and the Holy Spirit, which is the same; and delightful it is to feel it the same, amongst other nations and languages. It is confirming to faith o find the children of God in every place looking only to the same Savior, and built upon the same foundation.

"I wish I had power to convey to you an idea of our present interesting and curious situation. In the first place, I must introduce you to the room I am sitting in. It is perfectly unique. I should think the floor had never been really cleaned. It is filled with old boxes, and bottles, and pictures, and medicines, and books, but every thing is in its place. Two little beds are stuck up in each corner, and there are a few old chairs, &c. The window looks upon the tops of the mountains, near which we are,—separated from the world; but this is a spot highly favored, remarkably illuminated by the blessed light of the Gospel. I must now tell you of our journey here, and arrival.

"On Saturday morning, after an early breakfast, we left Strasbourg. I was rather sorry to quit our comfortable hotel, where I began to feel a little settled, and the place, as a *town*, pleased me. We soon left the high road, and as there were no more post-houses, we took a pair of horses to make our way as well as we could through the mountains. The roads were not quite so bad as I expected, yet their narrowness, and the steep precipice on one side, made me nervous. But we were charmed by the interest and beauty of the scenery:—before we had gone far we found the valleys luxuriant in vines and fine trees; a mountain river running through the valley, and presenting different views in every turn of the road. F. and I both thought we had never seen more exquisite *home* scenery. The postilion lost his way, and led us up a delicious valley. Though we enjoyed the scenery, our situation was not very pleasant, and we were anxious to arrive early; for we went perfect strangers, without any introduction, or having given any warning, but we felt confidence in going amongst Christian people. Having reached the right road again, we entered the *pass* leading into the Ban de la Roche; it was exceedingly interesting; we were upon the famous road, dug out of the rock, made by Mr. Oberlin himself, and his parishioners, for before he came the place was almost inaccessible.

"However good the roads were in comparison, I could not be satisfied to stay in the carriage, so we walked on to a very romantic little village, where Mr. Legrand and his family live, intimate friends of Mr. Oberlin. I fear you have not seen the book he wrote about Mr. O. and this place;* it gives great interest to it. It is really wonderful what he has effected. We inquired for their house. Mrs. Legrand was pointed out to us; she had a fine open countenance, but was dressed in a far commoner manner than any of our maids, who would appear like ladies in this place The women here are a hundred years at least behind us in luxury and fashion, and outward

* Letters to the Baron de Gerando, on the Agriculture of the Ban de la Roche, from which extracts have been given in this work.

appearance; such simplicity I never saw. I will now introduce you to the Legrands, one of the most cheerful and happy families one often sees. Their house is complete in its way, and full of comfort for a foreign habitation. The father and mother, with their two sons, both married to weet women, live together. They seemed beaming with goodness and happiness; evidently most domestic, and I should trust religious people, devotedly attached to Mr. Oberlin, their friend and minister, for whose sake they settled in this place.

"After this pleasant introduction to the Legrands, we again set off for Mr. Oberlin's, a mile and a half further, (a romantic walk through the valley,) accompanied by Mr. Legrand. On the way we met this most venerable and striking man—the perfect picture of what an old man and minister should be. He received us cordially, and we soon felt quite at ease with him. We all proceeded together towards his house, which stands on the top of a hill surrounded by trees and cottages; if we live to return, you shall see my sketch of it. In consequence of my ignorance of French, and the fatigue of our journey, I felt quite confused on our first arrival. I cou d see nothing like a mistress in the house; but an old woman, called Louisa, dressed in a long woollen jacket and black cotton cap, came to welcome us, and we afterwards found that she is an important person at the Ban de la Roche; she is mistress, housekeeper, intimate friend, *maid of all work*, school-mistress, entertainer of guests, and, I should think, assistant minister, though we have not yet heard her in this capacity. Besides Louisa, the son-in-law and daughter, and their six children live here, two young girls, protegés, and two more maids out of the parish. Mr. Graff, the son-in-law, is a minister and a very excellent man. There is much religion and simplicity both in him and his wife; but she is so devoted to the children that we seldom see her. We were ushered into the dining-room, where stood the table spread for supper; a great bowl of pottage—a pewter plate and spoon for every body:—the luxury of a common English cottage is not known here. But we see the fruits and feel the blessed effects of religion in its simplest form; it is a great privilege to be here, and I trust will be truly useful to us.

"Tuesday.—We are become more acquainted with this extraordinary people. They are as interesting as they are uncommon. I much regret that I cannot talk more fluently with them; yet I get on as well as I can, and have had a good deal of pleasing communication with them. I only hope you will read Owen's letters, with the description of his visit on a Sunday to this place it will give you an interest in our present situation. Also, in the Appendix of the First Bible Society Report, read Mr. Oberlin's letter. I never knew so well what the *grace* of courtesy was till I saw him. He treats the poorest people and even the children, with an affectionate respect. For instance, his courtesy, kindness, and hospitality to our postilion were quite amusing. He pulled his hat off when we met him, took him by the hand, and treated him with really tender consideration. He is, I think, more than eighty—one of the handsomest old men I ever remember to have seen—still vigorous in mind and spirit—delighting in his parish—full of fervent charity. He has talked a great deal to Mr. Cunningham. The meals are really amusing:—we all sit down to the same table, maids and all, one great dish of pottage or boiled spinach, and a quantity of salad and potatoes, upon which they chiefly live, being placed in the middle. He shakes hands with all the little children as he passes them in the street, speaking particularly to them individually:—it is quite wonderful to see the effect and polish which this sort of treatment and manner has had upon these people, uncultivated and uncivilized as they were before, from all accounts. I never met with any thing like the cultivation of mind amongst *poor* people. They have been taught a variety of things which have enlarged and polished their minds; besides religion—music, geography, drawing, botany, &c. My sketching has been quite a source of amusement in the parish, and my sketch-book handed about from one poor person to another.* If you go into a cottage they quite expect you will eat and drink with them; a clean cloth is laid upon the table, washed almost as white as milk, and the new milk and the wine,† and the

* As I was one day sketching upon the mountain, a group of poor peasant women attracted my attention, and I begged one of them to stand still for a few moments, that I might sketch her in the costume of her country. "Ah! Madam," she replied, smiling, "you shall sketch me. I should like you to have a picture of me in your book, because you will then be led to remember me, and perhaps to *pray* for me."

† The usual wine of the country, called *kirschen-wasser* is distilled from the fruit of the wild cherry.

great loaf of bread are brought out; yet they are in reality exceedingly poor. Their beds also look so clean and good that they would astonish our poor people. In some respects I think they are decidedly cleaner than our poor. Their dress is simple to the greatest degree. The women and girls all dress alike, even down to the very little children. They wear caps of dark cotton, with black ribbon, and the hair bound closely under. Every body—maids, children, poor, and rich, call Mr. Oberlin their "dear father," and never was there a more complete father of a large family. We breakfast at seven; the family upon potatoes boiled with milk and water—a little coffee is provided for us. We dine at twelve, and sup at half-past seven. Every thing is in the most primitive style. I never saw such people for not taking money. It is almost impossible to pay any body for any service they do for you. In our visits to the poor we have been afraid of offering them money; but we feel anxious to throw in some assistance towards the many important objects which Mr. Oberlin is carrying on amongst his people. It is almost past belief what he has done, and with *very limited* means. Three poor dear women are noted for their benevolence; one especially, who is a widow herself with several children, has taken to support and bring up three orphan children; and she has lately taken another from no other principle than abounding Christian charity. One seldom meets with such shining characters. Mr. O. told Mr. Cunningham the other day he did not know how to pay Louisa, for nothing hurt her so much as offering her money. Nothing can be more devoted to his service, and in the most disinterested manner. Her character has impressed me very much. We had a delightful walk to a church about two miles distant, on Sunday morning; the numbers of poor, flocking from the distant villages, dressed in their simple and neat costume, formed a striking object in the scene. It happened to be the Sunday Mr. O. goes to the next parish, where his son has him to assist in giving prizes to the school children.

"Wednesday evening.—The poor charm me. I never met with any like them; so much spirituality, humility, and cultivation of mind, with manners that would do honor to a court; yet the homely dress and the simplicity of the peasant are not lost. The state of the schools, the children, and the poor in general, is quite extraordinary, and as much exceeds our parish as ours does the most neglected.

"We have spent our time in the following manner: Since Sunday the mornings have been very wet; we have therefore been chiefly shut up in our own room, reading, writing, and drawing; the eldest of the Graffs, (Marie) a sweet girl, is a good deal with me, to read and to talk to me. The children and young people in the house are becoming fond of me; our being here is quite a gaiety and amusement to them. About three o'clock Mr. Legrand comes for us, to take us different excursions, &c. He seems to us one of the kindest persons we ever met with, full of conversation; nothing can exceed the torrent of words they all have. The old gentleman delights in talking to F—, and tells him every thing about himself, his family, his parishes, &c. Our room joins his library, and all the family are free to enter whenever they like. The whole system is most amusing, interesting and useful. It is a capital example, and instructive for the minister of a parish. I have felt it very enlarging and good for us to be here. There is a spirit of good fellowship and kindness amongst all the peopl that is quite delightful. The longer we have been here, the more we have been struck with the uncommon degree of virtue which exists amongst them. On Monday evening, after sketching Legrand's house, we were taken to the cottage of Sophia Bernard, where we found the table spread in the most complete manner for our tea, a luxury we had not enjoyed since we left England. Here we passed some time, eating, talking, and reading the Bible; and it ended with prayer, by Sophia Bernard, in a sweet and feeling manner. We then had a charming walk through the valley home.

"Tuesday.—In the afternoon we ascended towards the very top of the mountains, to another of his villages, where we again found some delightful women, and a capital school. This afternoon we have been drinking tea with the Legrands; so comfortable and complete a house and family is rarely to be met with in any country. The three pairs have each the most complete little dwelling, but in the same house. Our intercourse with them has been truly pleasant; they have treated us with real Christian kindness. Farewell, for to-night, my dearest sisters, may every blessing be with you!

* * * * * *

* * * * * *

"Colmar, Friday evening.—Our scene is again quite changed:—we are returned to the common world; and I now find myself over a comfortable fire at a good hotel, which is quite a luxury after the *primitive* fare of the Ban de la Roche. I believe Mr. Cunningham would have suffered, if we had continued to live much longer upon pottage and potatoes. There was but little indulgence for the body, though we were treated with genuine hospitality. They live sadly in the clouds. The sun does not appear very often to shine upon them. I never was so struck with the difference of climate as I was to-day, in coming down into the plains. It poured with rain for the last day or two; and all yesterday, in the mountains, every thing was soaked with wet; but on entering the plains the dust began to fly. Delightful and uncommon as is this retreat, I must acknowledge we have rather enjoyed the comforts of the town, and the conveniences of this place. It would be a trial to me to live surrounded and buried by mountains. I could not help rather feeling for Marie Graff, who is sensible of her privations. However, they are happy and contented, and highly blessed; and it is a great privilege to have passed this time with them; an event which must always be valuable through life. We parted from the excellent old man with many kisses, in the full spirit of Christian love; and the same with the rest of the family. We left them very early, accompanied by many of the family, and proceeded to Foudai, where the Legrands live. Here we breakfasted, and parted with many tears on their part. They are a most warm-hearted people. We then proceeded over such a road as would astonish our Norfolk and Suffolk friends. However, I am thankful that we got through safely. I am getting more bold, and can bear the precipices much better than at first. We passed some beautiful country, but whilst on the heights, the rain and mist were so great we could not see much.

"The thoughts of the Ban de la Roche, an the impression of this day, have been very pleasant to me, and I have a secret satisfaction and comfort in the prospect of getting to Basle, where I trust I shall have the great consolation of hearing from you."

* * * * * *

* * * * * *

The following extract, from a letter addressed by Mrs. Rauscher to the Paris Bible Society, presents a delightful picture of the good effects resulting from the instructions and example of her beloved parent, and from an education founded on the Holy Scriptures. It also speaks of the death of Sophia Bernard, an event which happened in the spring of 1822, about two years after the visit alluded to, in the preceding interesting letter.

This letter is dated March 14, 1826.

"Our parish has now possessed the Holy Scriptures for more than a century, and they form the basis of daily instruction in the schools. In addition to this, the young people have long been in the habit of receiving religious instruction from their pastor, so that a gradual and imperceptible improvement, resembling the growth of plants in a well cultivated garden, has taken place. You may form some estimate of their mora. progress, by the spirit of charity which manifests itself on occasion of the death of a poor father or mother leaving a numerous family; and by the eagerness with which the relations, friends, or neighbors of the deceased, take charge of the children, not to treat them as strangers and dependants, but as members of their own household. These noble actions do not arise from any fixed methodical rules, nor are they confined to any particular epoch; but are owing to the instructions of the good pastor, and to the excellent regulations which he has led his parishioners to adopt.

"This delightful spirit of benevolence particularly manifests itself also, in the eager alacrity with which the young people assist the old and feeble in their rural labors. No sooner are their own tasks completed in the evening, than the signal is given, and they set off to execute in concert some labor, which, by its charitable object, becomes a recreation. Is a new cottage to be built—the young people take upon themselves the task of collecting the materials together, and of assisting in its erection. Does it happen that a poor man loses his cow—his only support—the whole parish subscribe and raise a sum sufficient to replace it. Is a poor man visited with a misfortune of any kind—he is not the only sufferer—for all his neighbors participate in his affliction, as the Apostle says, 'If one member suffer, all the members suffer with it.' 1 Cor. 12: 26.

"These admirable works are doubtless effected by the influence of the Holy Spirit from on high, and by that spirit of Christian benevolence which the attentive and constant perusal of the Holy Scriptures cannot fail to inculcate.

"I will just mention as a single instance, among many others, of the transforming power of religion, that one young woman refused to marry, that she might devote her time, her talents, and her strength, to works of benevolence; and, allowing herself only the bare necessaries of life, she presented the fruits of her assiduous and unremitting industry to the excellent and pious institutions of the present day: she also sold all that she thought she could do without, and gave the produce to such objects as she believed calculated to advance the kingdom of our adorable Lord and Savior.

"The excellent Sophia Bernard, after whom you inquire, left her dwelling here below to inhabit a brighter mansion, about four years since, to the great regret of the whole parish, and of the inhabitants of the adjacent villages, who, though of a different religious denomination, considered that they had lost in her a mother, consoler, and comforter.

"Catharine Scheidecker and Maria Miller still live, though the former is very infirm.* They both continue to walk in the path of Gospel truth; endeavoring to follow the steps of their Divine Master, and praying to him continually for the salvation of their families, and that of all the inhabitants of their parish, as well as for every individual living. Both are poor in the

* She died in the autumn of 1826, and has doubtless received the "crown of glory" promised to those who are "faithful unto death."

wealth of this world, but rich in faith; and they take every opportunity of evincing their gratitude to God, whose love is shed abroad in their hearts.

"My venerable father sends you the salutation of a friend and brother in Christ Jesus our Lord, and implores the blessing of Almighty God upon you, and the labors of your society. He longs for the joyful period, when, released from his narrow prison-house of clay, he may enter upon that happiness which is to be acquired only through the merits of the Son of God, whose name is the 'Wonderful, Counsellor, the Prince of Peace.'"

I have already stated that it was the practice in the Ban de la Roche to meet on a particular evening, at stated periods, to read the Scriptures and pray for the Divine blessing on various religious institutions, and afterwards to make a collection for them. The collections thus made, consisted of voluntary contributions according to the abilities of the donor, and the sums that were sometimes raised are truly astonishing; 290 francs having been at one time remitted to the Paris Bible Society, and on another occasion, the sum of 500, to the London Committee, in furtherance of the same object.

The following extract is taken from a letter addressed by Mr. Daniel Legrand to Professor Kieffer. It is dated July 17, 1825.

"As all that our venerable patriarch receives and possesses, is only employed for the advancement of the kingdom of his Divine Master, he has again remitted to me 100 francs, desiring me to forward them to the Bible Society at Paris

His Louisa, (the name of his faithful housekeeper,) has added to it ten francs for the same purpose, and ten for the Missionary Society at Paris. She has a single field, and this is the amount of the rent. May the Lord put a peculiar blessing upon it!"

It would be almost repetition to say that these contributions towards *public* institutions did not prevent the inhabitants of the Steinthal from appropriating large sums to charitable societies nearer home. Their beneficence was not, however, confined to their immediate vicinity; for the Foundation for Protestant Theological Students at Strasbourg, the Reformed Theological Society at Montauban, and particularly the Protestant Institution for the Education of Poor Children of the Neuhof, near Strasbourg, were indebted to Oberlin and his people for much efficient assistance.

What can we add to facts so full of eloquence? Whilst contemplating the rich blessings which Oberlin disseminated around him, and which the pervading influence of his example so greatly augmented, we can only earnestly hope that the "centre" of Christian benevolence being once moved, "circle after circle" may succeed, and tenfold good be effected.

"Blessed is the man that trusteth in the Lord, and whose hope the Lord is. For he shall be as a tree planted by the waters, and that spreadeth out her roots by the river, and shall not see when heat cometh, but her leaf shall be green; and shall not be careful in the year of drought, neither shall cease from yielding fruit."—Jeremiah 17: 7, 8.

CHAPTER X.

Oberlin's last illness and death—Letter respecting Louisa Schepler found after his decease—His funeral—Prayer delivered upon that occasion—Fragments of an address to his parishioners—Conclusion.

Towards the latter part of Oberlin's life, the infirmities of age precluded his discharging the greater part of his pastoral functions, and he was therefore compelled to delegate the charge to his son-in-law, Mr. Graff, being able to do little more than occupy himself in constant prayers for his beloved flock.* That no individual might be omitted in his intercessions at the throne of grace, he used in the morning to take his church register of baptisms in his hand, and to pray, at stated intervals during the day, for every person whose name was there mentioned, as well as for the community at large. At all periods of his residence in the Ban de la Roche, Oberlin had a deep feeling of the value of intercessory prayer; and so alive was he upon this point, and so fearful lest he should omit any one whom he particularly wished to remember, that he wrote the names of such persons in chalk upon the black door of his chamber.

* In consequence of an apoplectic attack, Mr. Graff was compelled to relinquish his pastoral duties in the Ban de la Roche soon after Oberlin's decease, and to remove, with his wife and children, to Strasbourg, where he now resides. Mr. Rauscher is his successor, and occupies the parsonage house at Waldbach. Louisa Schepler lives with him and his family.

His strength had greatly diminished; his figure indeed was not bent, but symptoms of infirmity had made their appearance, and his white locks announced advancing age. He no longer left his home but from necessity, and devoted more time than formerly to the labors of his study. Several essays, on various subjects, found since his decease, appear to have been written at this period, and a refutation of Cicero's work, 'De Senectute,' drawn up in 1825, was probably the last he attempted.

His last illness attacked him suddenly, and was of short duration. On Sunday, the 28th of May, 1826, he was seized with shiverings and faintings, which lasted till a late hour of the night. The whole of the two following days were passed in alternate consciousness and insensibility; but he often exclaimed, when his strength permitted, "Lord Jesus, take me speedily! Nevertheless, *thy* will be done!" On the evening of Tuesday, Mr. Daniel Legrand, who had been absent on a missionary excursion to Basle, came to see him. He appeared delighted at his return, and, tenderly embracing him, said in a distinct voice, and in an accent of paternal solicitude, "The Lord bless you, and all who are dear to you! May He be with you day and night!" On the Wednesday he appeared considerably weakened by the convulsions he had undergone, an the want of nourishment, as a few drops of water were all he had been able to taste; he however still intimated by signs, when he was unable to speak, the tender affection which he felt for his children, his friends, his faithful Louisa, and all the members of his flock.

During the night, between Wednesday and Thursday, the 1st of June, which was a very distressing one to his attendants, he continued almost incessantly to utter plaintive cries, as though in pain, although in intervals of ease he would seize the hand of either of his children who happened to be nearest to him, and press it to his heart. When Mr. Legrand arrived, at six o'clock in the morning, from Foudai, he had lost the use of speech, and his arms and legs had become cold and lifeless. He, however, recovered strength sufficient to take off his cap, join his hands, and raise his eyes for the last time towards heaven; his countenance, as he did so, beaming with faith, joy, and love.

After this effort his eyes closed, never again to open; but it was not till a quarter after eleven that his spirit forsook its mortal tenement, and that the passing bell announced to the inhabitants of the valley that they had lost the pastor, benefactor, and friend, who for nearly sixty years had so unceasingly labored and prayed for them.

It would be impossible to describe the grief which his loss occasioned: sorrow was depicted on every countenance; and not only in his own house, but in every cottage throughout his extensive parish, was his memory embalmed by the tears and regrets of those who had participated in his labors of love, or enjoyed the benefit which his unremitted kindness afforded.

His care for those who had any peculiar claims on his affection, extended even beyond the grave. He was particularly anxious to evince his gratitude to the excellent Louisa, who had faithfully served him during a period of fifty years; and the following sealed letter, in which he speaks of her good qualities, and begs his children to treat her as a sister, was opened a few days after his death. It is dated, Waldbach, August 2, 1811.

"My very dear Children,

"In leaving you, I commend to your care the faithful nurse who has brought you up—the indefatigable Louisa. The services which she has performed for our family are innumerable. Your dear mamma took her under her care before she had attained the age of fifteen; but, even at that early period, she rendered herself useful by her talents, her activity, and her industry. On the premature decease of your beloved parent, she became at once your faithful nurse, your careful instructress, and your adopted mother. Her zeal for doing good extended beyond the confines of our own family. Like a devoted servant of the Lord, she went into all the surrounding villages, where I sent her, to assemble the children together, to instruct them in God's holy will, to teach them to sing hymns, to direct their attention to the wonderful works of nature, to pray with them, and to communicate to them all the knowledge that she had herself derived from me and your mamma. This was not the labor of a moment; and the innumerable difficulties which opposed themselves to her benevolent employments would have discouraged a thousand others; for whilst on the one hand she had to contend with the wild and froward characters of the children, she had, on the other, to correct their *patois*, and, consequently, after having spoken to them in that dialect, which was necessary to make herself understood, to translate all she had said into French. The bad roads and the inclement weather, so frequent on these mountains, presented another difficulty; but neither sleet, nor rain, nor wind, nor hail, nor deep snows under foot, nor snow falling from above, detained her from her purpose; and when she returned in the evening, though exhausted, wet, and weary, and chilled with excessive cold, she would set herself to attend to my children, and to our household affairs. In this manner she devoted not only her time and abilities, but also her health, and all her bodily powers, to my service, and to the service of our God. For many years past indeed, her lungs have been injured, and her constitution absolutely ruined, by over fatigue, and by sudden transitions from heat to cold, and from cold to heat, having often, when warm with walking, crossed the snows and sank into them to such a depth as to be scarcely able to get out. She received a sufficient recompense, you will perhaps say, in the ample salary that I allowed her. No, dear children, no: since the death of your dear mother, I have never been able to prevail on her to accept the least reward for her services; she employed her own little property in doing good, and in the purchase of her scanty wardrobe; and it was always as a favor that she received from me some light articles of dress, and provisions, which I owed, notwithstanding, to her economy and good management. Judge, dear children, judge of the debt you have contracted, from her services to me, and how far you will ever be from repaying it.

"In times of sickness and affliction, how kindly has she watched over both you and me; how tenderly has she sought to mitigate our pains and to assuage our griefs! Once more I commend her to you. You will evince, by the care that you take of her, how much attention you pay t the last wish of a father, who has always en deavored to inspire you with feelings of gratitude and benevolence:—but, yes:—yes:—you will fulfil my wishes. You will be, in your turn, both individually and collectively, all that she has been to you, as far as your means, situation, and opportunity permit.

"Adieu, my very dear children, your papa,

"J. F. Oberlin."

So well disposed were Oberlin's children to fulfil this request, and to coincide in their father's views, that they offered Louisa an equal share of the little property he had left. This, however, she refused, asking nothing more than permission to remain an inmate of the family, and to be allowed to add the honored name of ***Oberlin*** to her own. "It is almost superfluous to say," writes one of his children, "that whilst a descendant of Oberlin's remains, Louisa shall want for nothing, at least, until they themselves are destitute."

Oberlin's funeral took place on the 5th of June During the four days that intervened between his decease, and the simple and affecting ceremony which consigned his remains to their last home, heavy clouds rested on the surrounding mountains, and the rain poured down in incessant torrents; this circumstance did not, however prevent the inhabitants of the Ban de la Roche, of all ages and conditions, nearer or more remote, from coming to pay a last tribute of respect to the remains of their "dear father," whose venerable countenance they were permitted to see through a glass lid, which, under the direction of Mr. Legrand, covered the coffin, which was placed in his study.

Early in the morning of the day fixed on for the interment, the clouds cleared away, and the sun shone with its wonted brilliancy. As they left the house, the president of the Consistory of Barr, the Rev. Mr. Jaeglé, placed the clerical robes of the late pastor on his coffin, the vice-president placed his Bible upon it, and the mayor affixed to the funeral pall the decoration of the Legion of, Honor. At the conclusion of this ceremony, ten or twelve young females, who had been standing around the bier, began to sing a hymn in chorus, and at two o'clock the procession took its departure, the coffin being borne by the mayors, elders, and official magistrates. In front of it, walked the oldest inhabitant of the Ban de la Roche, carrying a cross, which Louisa had given him, to plant on the tomb, and on which the words, ***Papa Oberlin***, were engraved in open letters.

So numerous was the concourse of people assembled on the occasion, that the foremost of the train had already reached the church of Foudai, where the interment was to take place, before the last had left the parsonage, although the distance was nearly two miles. The children of the different schools formed part of the melancholy procession, chanting, at intervals, sacred hymns, selected and adapted foı the occasion. At the moment of their approaching the village, a new bell, presented by Mr. Legrand in commemoration of this day of general mourning, was heard to toll for the first time, and to mingle its melancholy sound with that of all the bells in the valley. The burying-ground was surrounded by Roman Catholic women, all dressed in mourning, and kneeling in silent prayer. On arriving at the church, the coffin was placed at the foot of the altar, and as many persons entered as the little edifice would contain, though more than three-fourths of the company had to remain in the church-yard, and the adjoining lanes. Notwithstanding the pressure of so immense a multitude, the utmost order and solemnity prevailed. Several females, who could find room nowhere else, sat down on the steps of the altar, leaning with melancholy affection against the coffin, as though anxious to cling to the very ashes of one whom they had so much revered and loved. Many distinguished individuals were present on the occasion, and several Roman Catholic priests, dressed in their canonicals, took their seats among the members of the Consistory, and evidently participated in the general grief. Mr. Jaeglé then mounted the pulpit, and commenced the service by reading a manuscript of Oberlin's, dated 1784, and found among his papers after his death. It is filled with so many expressions of ardent attachment, and intercession for his beloved parishioners, that I cannot refrain from inserting it.

Fragment, written by Oberlin, in 1784.

"I was born at Strasbourg on the last day of August, 1740, and baptized on the 1st of September, in the church of St. Thomas.

"During my infancy and my youth, God often vouchsafed to touch my heart, and to draw me to himself. He bore with me in my repeated backslidings, with a kindness and indulgence hardly to be expressed.

"I arrived in this parish, in the capacity of pastor, on the 30th of March, 1767, when twenty-seven years of age.

On the 6th of July, in the year following, God united me to that beloved woman, whom, (after having received many services from her hands,) you, six months ago, followed to the grave. Her name was Madeleine Salomè Witter. I have had nine children. Two, who are yet living, were born in the Ban de la Roche; the others at Strasbourg. Two have already entered Paradise; and seven remain in this world. On the 18th of January last, ten weeks after her last confinement, my wife, although in apparently good health, was suddenly taken from me. Upon this occasion, as upon a thousand others in the course of my life, notwithstanding my overwhelming affliction, I was upheld by God's gracious assistance, in a remarkable manner.

"I have had all my life a desire, occasionally a very strong one, to die, owing, in some degree, to the consciousness of my moral infirmities, and of my frequent derelictions. My affection for my wife and children, and my attachment to my parish, have sometimes checked this desire, hough for short intervals only. I had, about a year since, some presentiment of my approaching end. I did not pay much attention to it at the time, but, since the death of my wife, I have frequently received unequivocal warnings of the same nature. Millions of times have I besought God to enable me to surrender myself with entire and filial submission to his will, either to live or to die; and to bring me into such a state of resignation, as neither to wish, nor to say, nor to do, nor to undertake any thing, but what He who only is wise and good, sees to be best.

"Having had such frequent intimations of my approaching end, I have arranged all my affairs, as far as I am able, in order to prevent confusion after my death. For my dear children, I fear nothing; but, as I always greatly preferred being useful to others to giving them trouble, I suffer much from the idea that they may occasion sorrow or anxiety to the friends who take charge of them. May God abundantly reward them for it! With regard to the children themselves, I have no anxiety, for I have had such frequent experience of the mercy of God towards myself, and place such full reliance upon his goodness, his wisdom, and his love, as to render it impossible for me to be at all solicitous about them. Their mother was, at a very early age, deprived of her parents, but she was, notwithstanding, a better Christian than thousands who have enjoyed the advantage of parental instruction.

"Besides this, I know that God hears our prayers; and ever since the birth of our children, neither their mother nor I have ceased to suppli cate Him to make them faithful followers cf Jesus Christ, and laborers in his vineyard.

"And thou, O my dear parish! neither will God forget nor forsake thee. He has towards thee, as I have often said, thoughts of peace and mercy. All things will go well with thee. Only cleave thou to Him, and leave Him to act. Oh! mayest thou forget my name, and retain only that of Jesus Christ, whom I have proclaimed to thee. He is thy pastor; I am but his servant. He is that good master, who, after having trained and prepared me from my youth, sent me to thee, that I might be useful. He alone is wise, good, almighty, and merciful; and as for me, I am a poor, feeble, wretched man.

"O, my friends, pray, in order that you may all become the beloved sheep of his pasture. There is salvation in no other than Jesus Christ; and Jesus loves you, seeks you, and is ready to receive you. Go to Him, just as you are, with all your sins and all your infirmities. He alone can deliver you from them, and can heal you. He will sanctify and perfect you. Dedicate yourselves to Him! Whenever any of you die, may you die in Him; and may I meet you, and accompany you with songs of triumph, in the mansions of felicity, before the throne of the Lamb!

"Adieu, dear friends, adieu! I have loved you much; and even the severity which I have ometimes deemed it necessary to exercise, has arisen from my earnest desire to contribute to your happiness.

"May God reward you for your services, your good deeds, and the deference and submission which you have shown towards his poor unworthy servant. May He forgive those who have pained me by opposition. They doubtless knew not what they did.

"O, my God! let thine eye watch over my dear parishioners; let thine ear be open to hear them; thine arm be extended to succor and protect them. Lord Jesus! thou hast intrusted this parish to my care, feeble and miserable as I am. Oh, suffer me to commend it to thee, to resign it into thy hands. Give it pastors after thine own heart. Never forsake it. Overrule all things for its good. Enlighten them, guide them, love them, bless them all; and grant that the young and old, the teachers and the taught, pastors and parishioners, may all in due time meet together in thy paradise! Even so! Father, Son, and Holy Spirit!—even so. Amen!"

After the solemn reading of this pathetic document, which was evidently intended for Oberlin's dying charge, Mr. Jaeglé read the following verses from the 103d Psalm:

"Bless the Lord, O my soul: and all that is within me, bless his holy name. Bless the Lord, O my soul, and forget not all his benefits; who forgiveth all thine iniquities; who healeth all thy diseases; who redeemeth thy life from destruction; who crowneth thee with loving-kindness and tender mercies." And the 14th verse of the 7th chapter of the Book of Revelations, which Oberlin had himself selected to serve as texts to the discourse to be pronounced at his funeral, conscious, as he often declared himself to be, that however numerous and useful the good works he had performed, they needed "to be washed in the blood of Christ."

The Rev. Mr. Jaeglé then delivered a discourse, which was listened to with the profoundest attention. On its conclusion the whole congregation knelt down, and repeated the following rayer:

"Almighty God! our days are in thy hands, thou governest all our destinies by thy supreme wisdom. By thy will we enter on this life, and we return to the dust at thy word. Thanks be to thee for the sublime consolations given us in the Gospel of thy Son, who has come to bring life and immortality to light; consolations without which we should be given up to despair; when those whom we love are snatched away by death, or when it approaches us with its terrors. We pray that wisdom—that the love of that which is good emanating from thee—source of all good, may accompany us in our journey to the eternal world, that we may pass our days as children submissive and faithful, with a consciousness of having followed thy commandments, and having preferred the salvation of our souls to the deceitful interests and pleasures of earth.

"Oh Lord, our God, thou hast called to thyself our excellent pastor—our beloved father; thou hast given him a place in those eternal mansions which are prepared for the righteous. Oh! hat his memory may be preserved among us, that the love of Thee and thy Son, with which he has endeavored to inspire us—that the love of religion without which there is neither peace nor hope, may never be effaced from our hearts. Then shall we contemplate again in a better world, when the sleep of death shall have closed our eyelids, him whom we now mourn in this moment of loss, and then shall we rejoice together with him in that eternal salvation to which God has called us through our Savior Jesus Christ.—AMEN!"

Another hymn having been sung, the coffi was conveyed to the church-yard, where the grave was dug on a little eminence on one side of the edifice, under the shade of a weeping willow, planted over the tomb of Henry Oberlin.

The Rev. Mr. Braunwald, pastor of Goxviller, and vice-president of the Consistory of Barr, then delivered the following address:

"My Christian brethren,

"WE are brought to endure a great and afflictive loss: the good father Oberlin has left us; he has finished in peace his earthly career. Around his tomb I see the faithful of the two parishes of the Ban de la Roche: the faithful of Waldbach and of Rothau, unite their sorrows and their tears with those of the children and numerous friends of the venerable dead. If, penetrated with sentiments of love and admiration for the venerable pastor of Waldbach, I speak in this day of grief, I know well, my brethren, that it is not in my power worthily to portray to yo the exalted viitues and the estimable qualities oi the man we deplore.

"Our consistorial church has lost in this aged, revered and zealous pastor, a man distinguished by his talents and his virtues; the parish of Waldbach, the Ban de la Roche in general, a benefactor, a father the most affectionate—his family—his friends, their model, the source of their felicity, and human nature one of its brightest ornaments. What a spirit pure and elevated, what simplicity, what affability, what complacency, what rectitude, what candor have we to admire in this blessed man! More than four-score years the venerable Oberlin devoted his wasting powers to the glory of his God, and to his latest sigh, he implored the blessings of the Eternal upon this dear parish, centre of all his affections.

"What tender solicitude to cherish the flock confided to his care and guidance! Worthy servant of his divine Master, zealous successor of the apostles, he devoted himself entirely to benevolence after their example. During fifty-nine years he has devoted all his physical and intellectual powers—all the time of his laborious life to the improvement of this interesting region: civilization already commenced by the pious Stouber, with disinterestedness the most noble, with a firmness most invincible, with a zeal equal to any undertaking, he has, in voluntarily sacrificing his fortune, done every thing for the security, the comfort and well-being of the inhabitants of your humble dwellings. It is to the good pastor Stouber and to Oberlin, your father, that you owe your churches and your schools; it is Oberlin who has formed your instructors; it is he who has covered your naked and arid rocks with fertile soil; it is he who has changed all these hamlets into flourishing villages; it is he who labored with you to repair and widen your roads; it is he who testified a noble compassion for your poor, who nourished them in times of scarcity;

it is he who has succored the widows and the orphans; who has protected the outcasts; it is he —but I forbear: your hearts speak these recollections, you yourselves will finish this feeble picture of what he has done for your prosperity. In his philanthropy, Oberlin never limited himself by contracted views, he made no distinction in forms of worship, persuaded as he was that intolerance dishonored charity.

"What was he in the bosom of his family? Ah, who could see him there without being touched, moved, melted! What was he to his dear companion; to thee, valiant Frederic; to thee, pious Henry, to you blessed Fidelity, to you zealous Wolff; to you our friends, Charles and Sophia, Henrietta and Graff, to you excellent Graff, who, in performing the duties of a filial piety, would relieve the good father of all his painful functions; to you Louisa and Witz, Frederic and Rauscher; to you his grand-children; to you excellent Louisa Schepler?—What a spouse, what a father and grand-father!—What harmony, what unity, what love, what filial piety in this happy family?—What was he to his numerous friends? to thee noble, patriarchal and pious family of Foudai, to you worthy and respectable Legrand?

"The pious Oberlin rekindled the torch of faith, he brightened religion in our regions. Still more than for the welfare of this life, did he exert himself for the salvation of your immortal souls. The glory of all his efforts, the price of all his solicitudes was your spiritual welfare, believers of the parish of Waldbach!

"With what warmth, what energy, what simplicity, what perseverance he preached to you the gospel of Christ, the precious gift of heaven, the truths of religion engraven in your hearts! He taught you to find in the Holy Bible, in the precepts of Jesus Christ, the remedy for all your evils, the refuge from all your miseries, the real source of pleasures the most pure, of happiness in the life that now is, and of that which is to come. It is the gospel in possession, that purifies, enlightens, consoles, and sanctifies you. Is it not he who by his word and example has nourished in your hearts the love of God and man; is it not he who has conducted you near to the Redeemer who suffered for us—to this pre-eminent virtue of the Christian—to this fervent faith which constitutes the felicity of the Christian, who has exhibited to you our adorable Savior in the celestial mansions, where he waits for us; where he is gone to prepare a place for us; is it not he who has so often exhorted you to labor for the meat which endureth unto everlasting life? John 14: 2, and 6: 27.

"It is to your worthy patriarch that you owe this word of grace; it is he who has distributed to you this manna which nourished your souls; it is he who has carried the gospel into your houses and into the cabins of so many of the poor beyond this parish. Oh! my brethren, draw from this treasury which is inexhaustible, which enriches in proportion as one draws! Bless the name of Oberlin, bless the memory of this righteous man, who could say in truth with St. Paul, the great apostle: 'I have served the Lord with all humility of mind, and with many tears and temptations; I have kept back nothing that was profitable unto you, but have showed you, and have taught you publicly, and from house to house, testifying repentance toward God, and faith toward our Lord Jesus Christ. Nothing moves me, neither count I my life dear unto myself, so that I might finish my course with joy, and the ministry which I have received of the Lord Jesus, to testify the gospel of the grace of God. Among you, I have gone preaching the kingdom of God, wherefore I take you to record this day, that I am pure from the blood of all men. For I have not shunned to declare unto you all the counsel of God. I have coveted no man's silver, or gold, or apparel.' [Acts 20.] Do you not discover in these traits the image of your venerable pastor Oberlin?

"And, my brethren, what has he done for the propagation of the holy religion of Jesus Christ, for the propagation of our sacred volumes? Speak, ye Bible Societies of Strasbourg, of Paris, and of London! Speak, ye institutions of the Missions of Basle and of Paris! What sums he has contrived to amass—what donations he succeeded in directing to these pious Societies, that the Bible might be universally spread, that the doctrine of Christ might penetrate even climates the most inclement, and nations the most barbarous; that God and the Savior might be adored by every inhabitant of earth! How delightful to him, to see, in running over the reports of Bible and Missionary Societies, the blessing of the Lord descend upon his work!

"His career, full of trials, privations, and dangers, his long-suffering, has displayed his whole soul, and those sublime virtues of which it was the focus. A patience that nothing could divert, a resignation thoroughly Christian, have always rendered him perfectly superior to all his evils. He had contemplated death with a steady eye, with the composure and serenity of a saint. In taking his leave of earth, he committed himself to his God, he prayed for his family, his friends, his parish, and while he blessed them, his soul was snatched to heaven. Oberlin has left us; his death was the recompense of a life replete with goodness, with actions righteous and generous.

"What a throng in his funeral train, what grief, what tears! Two parishes, eight communes, this crowd of friends and strangers, all declare with one voice—to a good man we render our last respects—it is Oberlin, our father, our benefactor whom we mourn; friendship, veneration, gratitude, have brought us to this tomb! His ashes repose in the midst of you, kind inhabitants of the Ban de la Roche. This tomb, which incloses his mortal remains, shall be to us all a sacred spot. We will show it to our children, and say, Here sleeps Oberlin our father! He has made us happy—his image is graven in our hearts—the love is stronger than death—Waldbach shall be a lasting monument to his glory—the names of Oberlin and Waldbach will be for ever united in the memory of mankind.

"Adore the ways of Providence, my brethren. In the place of the venerable father, the Lord has given us the worthy husband of the daughter of Oberlin, the friend he so dearly loved, a servant afte: God's own heart. It was the choice of the ex:ellent father, and the choice is a new proof of the care of heaven over this flock.

With perfect confidence did Oberlin commit into the hands of this successor the sacred deposit of which his divine Master had given him the charge. Oh yes, Christians, adore this Providence which unites and separates us—afflicts and consoles us—enter into his views, complete his designs. Be joined in the bonds of that charity, which is the greatest of all the graces. Let us love during this mortal life, and again in that to come let us love. Let us love in God in whose bosom we shall one day find ourselves eternally reunited, if we serve him faithfully here below. Vow to the God of all grace, a resignation complete, a faith unshaken—and may the Father of mercies be the consolation and support of the afflicted family, of the friends of the venerable dead, of this parish filled with mourning!

"Adieu, venerable Oberlin! in heavenly mansions thou art reaping that which thou hast sown —thy works do follow thee; delivered from every evil, thy Lord will say to thee, 'I know thy works, thy charity, thy faith, thy patience.' [Rev. 2: 19.] Adieu, noble friend, adieu respected father! never shall thy image be effaced from our hearts—ever shalt thou be the object of our veneration; thy memory—the memory of the righteous shall be blessed for ever.—Amen."

M. Bedel, a physician of Schirmeck, then stepped forward amongst the crowd, and pronounced a short eulogy on the deceased; and amidst the tears of the assembled multitude, which formed, perhaps, the most eloquent funeral oration, his remains were consigned to the grave.

In delineating the character of this extraordinary man, we have not, it is true, had to trace his steps, with those of the philanthropic Howard, through the desolate regions of Russia, nor to witness his expiring sighs in the dreary wilds of Tartary; we have not had to follow him, with the pious and indefatigable Martyn, across the sunny plains of Persia, to communicate the gla tidings of salvation to the benighted heathen, nor to see him, regardless of his own shattered health, sacrifice his life to the glory of Christ amongst the nations of the East:—OBERLIN'S sphere of usefulness was at *home*.—But there, in the secluded recesses of his beloved Vosges, the benevolent ardor of Howard, and the self-denying zeal of Martyn, were eminently displayed.

To get good from heaven, and to do good on earth, constituted, indeed, the sole aim of his life, and constrained the dedication of every talent and the consecration of every power to the service of his Lord and Master. Humility was intimately blended with his other Christian graces; and, deeply conscious of his own inability to advance one step in holiness, or to induce others to follow him in his path Zion-wards, without Divine assistance, he meekly depended on, and earnestly implored, the aid of God's Holy Spirit: repeatedly uttering his favorite maxim, "Nothing without God." So far from being actuated by the hope of reward for any personal worthiness, he disclaimed all merit of his own, and, firmly believing in the divinity, rested entirely on the propitiation of Jesus. "All to the Savior," was his constant motto, and constituted the moving principle of his exertions. "What," said he to a minister who visited him a short time before his last illness, "did not our dear Savior suffer for us?—Nothing then is difficult when we do it for *Him*. To Him let us wholly devote ourselves."

Through the all-sufficiency of that Savior's atonement, he is now, undoubtedly, praising God in that kingdom of light and love, for which whilst on earth he so ardently longed; and, having exchanged the graces of time for the glories of eternity, is joining in the triumphant song of the "ten thousand times ten thousand:" "Worthy is the Lamb that was slain to receive power, and riches, and wisdom, and strength, and honor, and glory, and blessing."—"Blessing, and honor, and glory, and power, be unto Him that sitteth upon the thrcne, and unto the Lamb for ever and ever!'

THE END.

www.ingramcontent.com/pod-product-compliance
Lightning Source LLC
LaVergne TN
LVHW010256110826
845151LV00004B/1488

* 9 7 8 1 4 2 5 5 2 2 4 3 8 *